VICTORIAN
AMERICA

WENDELL GARRETT

VICTORIAN AMERICA

CLASSICAL ROMANTICISM
TO
GILDED OPULENCE

EDITED BY DAVID LARKIN

PRINCIPAL PHOTOGRAPHY BY PAUL ROCHELEAU

RIZZOLI
NEW YORK

For my daughter
Maria Clewes Garrett

Fama semper vivat

First published in the United States of America in 1993 by
RIZZOLI INTERNATIONAL PUBLICATIONS, INC.
300 Park Avenue South, New York, New York 10010

The photographs are by Paul Rocheleau
except for the following pages:
Helga Studio 61, 203, 230-33, 235, 250–55, 280–83
Michael Freeman 76, 76, 91
Victoria Mansion 134–41
Charles L. Norton 146–57
Richard Cheek 180–95
Olana 236–43
Antiques 245–48, 256–59
Steve Martin 260–63

Library of Congress Cataloging-in-Publication Data

Garrett, Wendell. D.
Victorian America: classical romanticism to gilded opulence
Wendell Garrett: edited by David Larkin
p. cm.
0847817474
1. Architecture, Domestic—United States.
2. Architecture, Victorian—United States.
3. Decoration and ornament—United States—Victorian style.
I. Larkin, David. II. Title.
NA7207.G37 1993
728'.373'097309034—dc20
93-10433

Design by David Larkin

Rizzoli Editor: Lois Brown

Printed and bound in Italy

CONTENTS

The Age of Romanticism in the Agrarian South

The Making of Modern America

THE NINETEENTH CENTURY opened with the election of Thomas Jefferson of Charlottesville, Virginia, as the third president of the United States; it closed with the assassination of President William McKinley of Canton, Ohio, by an anarchist at the Buffalo Exposition. It was a century of change accompanied by a furious pace of transformation and expansion. Americans had embarked on what George Washington himself called a "great experiment," and not everyone was sanguine about the outcome. Local pride and sectional animosities were strong, and there was doubt whether the thirteen former British colonies formed or would ever form a coherent nation. Of a total population of just under four million, more than a sixth were African-Americans held in slavery. Poor roads hindered the movement of men and of goods, and the economy, dominated by agriculture, was localized. As before the Revolution, imports and exports were closely tied to the mother country. Certain English travelers prophesied a dismal, brief, and factious future before the new nation tumbled into anarchy.

But there were more cheerful predictions, and these multiplied in volume and confidence as each year passed without bringing disaster. Their general theme was that the innocent New World had escaped from the immemorial strife and vice of the Old World. That American evolution was preordained had been an article of faith among the New England Puritans, and in secularized versions it continued to seem self-evident throughout the nineteenth century. The new nation was, in its own eyes, a different place. "America, North and South," Jefferson reiterated in 1823, "has a set of interests distinct from Europe, and peculiarly her own. She should therefore have a system of her own, separate . . . from that of Europe. While the last is laboring to become the domicile of despotism, our endeavor should surely be to make our hemisphere that of freedom." To this generation of Founding Fathers, emergent America represented an exciting experiment—a cosmic opportunity to spread the ideals of republicanism, Christianity, and technology across the world horizon. The shared American conviction was that the United States was unique in world history: in its origins, in its present structure, and in its destiny on a continent where opportunity was almost literally boundless. Americans, protected by the great oceans and the absence of formal European alliances, were free to grow, develop, and expand across the great empty continent.

The Jacksonian age witnessed the so-called rise of the common man. There was a surge of admiration and respect for the rude majority who seized control of the government by electing the hero of the Battle of New Orleans to the presidency. Property qualifications for voting were low (the two exceptions, of course, being women and African-Americans) and were virtually abolished in all states by 1830. In politics, the evidence suggests that a democratic spirit emerged that repudiated traditional notions of deference and position. The first six presidents, from George Washington to John Quincy Adams, all could be described as gentlemen; so could a majority of the men who sought to enter Congress and state legislatures. A marked change was signalized by the election of Andrew Jackson to the presidency in 1828, a "self-made" man (the expression dates from this era) as were several of his eminent political contemporaries: Daniel Webster, Henry Clay, Thomas Hart Benton, and his successor in the White House, Martin Van Buren. The presidency, said a Missouri newspaper in 1837, was "within the reach of the humblest urchin that roams the streets of our villages. . . . *Liberty and Equality* is the glorious motto of our republic."

Transition was the leading characteristic of the Victorian period. A new industrial society was being created out of the orderly society of Jefferson's agrarian democracy, and its creation involved the uprooting and transplanting of millions of people, drawing men off the land and raising new groups to power over the once powerful. Behind these profound changes and tumultuary years—beneficent to some, cataclysmic to others—lay a vast expansion of commerce, new methods of production based on the factory and the machine, and the new principle of *laissez-faire*, of unlimited competition in which the manufacturer bought his materials in the cheapest market and sold them in the highest. Nothing was left untouched in the process. The fixed relationships between the state and its citizens, the family, and the church began to crumble.

The faster tempo of this dynamic, freewheeling society revolutionized life in America. Until the Victorian period, the horse and the sailing vessel had set the pace. Now, within a very few years, the startling novelty of macadam roads, railroads, improved inland waterways, and ocean-going steamships impressed the Victorians with an intense awareness of speed—a sense of faster and more crowded living. This was a century of insatiable curiosity and restless energy. Their encounter with this new world must have impressed most Americans as the steamboat did Huckleberry Finn: "She was a big one, and she was coming in a hurry, too. . . . All of a sudden she bulged out, big and scary, with a long row of wide-open furnace doors shining like red-hot teeth." With startling speed a nation of sturdy farmers and small-town artisans learned the techniques of an industrial society. There was room for the jack-of-all-trades in the village but not in the factory, and specialist workmen replaced general artisans. Yet farming remained the main occupation of Americans during the Northwestern Surge, as land-hungry settlers broke through the Appalachians to seize the flat and later the rolling prairies to the west. The prairie land seemed to pulsate with energy, as this magical mix of improved farm machinery (the steel plow and McCormick reaper) and the intelligence, daring, and persistence of the farm people made the American heartland the granary of the world—a cornucopia of corn and wheat, of pork and beef. While northwestern farming surged and northeastern agriculture with Yankee resourcefulness adapted to change, much of the farming in the Deep South lagged behind. The institution of slavery was keeping the South excessively rural, with an unbalanced economy dominated by dangerous speculation in cotton, tobacco, and sugar. Walled in by poor communication and transportation, depleted soils, limited capital, lack of diversification, and a slower population growth, southerners lacked the incentive to break out of the pattern so long as rising prices for King Cotton brought prosperity for some of the larger plantation owners.

The Rise of the Cotton Kingdom

After the Revolution, tobacco was no longer a boom crop for southern planters. Erosion and soil exhaustion combined to disfigure the tidewater countryside, and with arable land in disrepair, many estates on the coastal plain were overstocked with slaves. But after the invention of the cotton gin in 1793, the tempo of life in the South quickened as slaveholders, optimistic and greedy for hard cash, believed that cotton was a profitable crop and slave labor the most economical means to cultivate it. To expand both their "Cotton Kingdom" and the productivity of plantations, planters pushed southwestward, settling on the rich virgin soils of the New South regions of the Gulf states. The cotton gin was a technological breakthrough that affected nearly every aspect of southern life, stimulating the growth of a materialistic spirit, a vast westward migration, an unbalanced economy, and, most unfortunate of all, the revitalization of the dying institution of slavery. Planter arrogance centered on the agricultural pre-eminence of the South, which South Carolina Senator James H. Hammond expressed flamboyantly in the Senate in 1858: "What would happen if no cotton was furnished for three years. . . . England would topple headlong and carry the whole civilized world with her, save the South. No, you dare not make war on cotton. No power on earth dares to make war on it. Cotton is King."

There were fundamental differences between North and South. While the political center in New England remained the town, plantation society revolved around the county unit. Urbanization and industrialization, which made such inroads into northern society, had little impact upon the plantation South. European immigrants avoided the region, as planters discouraged any influx of foreigners from a xenophobic impulse to preserve their own homogeneity. The economic differential between the two regions increased in these decades with the growth of manufacturing in New England and the boom in cotton in the Gulf states. The fundamental differences between North and South—incompatibilities accepted by both Yankees and planters, each arguing for his own superiority—were articulated by Thomas Jefferson. Northerners, he said, were "cool, sober, laborious, persevering, independent, jealous of their own liberties, and just to those of others, interested, chicaning, superstitious and hypocritical in their religion," while southerners were "fiery, voluptuary, indolent, unsteady, independent, zealous for their own liberties but trampling on those of others, generous, candid and without attachment or pretension to any religion but that of the heart." Southern distinctiveness was the product of the relationship between master and slave, affecting class relationships and social structures and defining the ideology of power that gave meaning to every action within the precapitalist social order of southern civilization.

Just as tobacco dominated the colonial South, so did cotton dominate most of the antebellum South. Short-staple cotton was a sturdy plant that could be grown in the hill country and the interior of the South wherever there were two hundred frostless days. The cotton belt very rapidly spread over a vast area from North Carolina to the south and southwest, all the way to eastern Texas. The southern states became the world's largest producer of raw cotton between 1820 and 1860, at the very time that worldwide demand for cotton cloth rose dramatically. From the beginning of the cotton trade until the Civil War, the great port to which cotton was shipped was Liverpool, the port of entry for Manchester, the textile center of Great Britain. Liverpool determined the price of cotton on the unstable world market, where prices fluctuated according to the different grades of the staple, economic panics, European wars, and overproduction. But, in general, these were years of economic prosperity for cotton planters, who in 1860 produced their greatest crop of over four and a half million bales, each one averaging about four hundred pounds. Despite the vagaries of cotton prices, profits from the white fiber lured planters to buy up vast lands and large numbers of slaves on generous credit. The Appalachian Mountains did not deter the advance of the cotton domain. As the lands of the Piedmont wore out, cotton planters moved with their slaves to the fertile lands of Alabama and Mississippi, and later to Arkansas and eastern Texas. The warm climate and rich lands of the lower Mississippi Valley and the Gulf Coast were ideally suited to the cotton plant, and from about 1835 to the Civil War, this area produced about 75 percent of all cotton grown in the United States. In the Deep South, cotton culture became almost synonymous with southern culture, and the society as well as the economy were forever marked by its presence.

The Cult of Romanticism

"Strictly, the Southerner," Henry Adams wrote in his *Education*, "had no mind; he had temperament." The literary taste of the people in the Old South turned to romantic works, particularly the novels of Sir Walter Scott, which reinforced the South's commitment to Gothic feudalism, to medieval chivalry, to make-believe tournaments, to an antique, gentlemanly way of life. Their contact with the romantic spirit came through the florid rhetoric of southern orators, the conservative orthodoxy of their evangelical religion and folk songs, and their concept of manly honor. This small group of planters at the apex of the social pyramid of the Old South mistakenly thought of themselves as descended from noble cavaliers who had migrated to the colonies during the colonial era, and they viewed themselves in the tradition of the eighteenth-century English country squires—living a life, not only of leisure and pleasure on vast landed estates, but also of *noblesse oblige*, particularly the obligation of public service in local affairs. The plantation legend and the South's construction of the "cavalier image" emerged to support the view that southerners were a distinct people, and these concepts became ingrained in the minds of both southerners and northerners before the Civil War.

"I am a Southern man," declared John C. Calhoun in one of his speeches in Congress. It was the defense of the South—that region which, as he saw it, he personally embodied—to which he devoted a good deal of his life. By the time Calhoun came to talk of the South, it had already been "codified," ascribed particular significances and perceived in terms of certain inherited mythologies. There was that familiar dream of a feudal society—an organic, hierarchical order changing very slowly and very little over time. This belief in a hierarchical system was the patriarchal model that found its summit and embodiment in what the writer William Gilmore Simms called "the Southern aristocrat—the true nobleman of that region." To southerners living in a region captured by the aura of romanticism, honor was important. If a southerner was insulted, lied about, or verbally attacked, his honor compelled him to challenge his adversary to a duel, in accordance with an elaborate *Code Duello* etiquette.

Closely connected to the high sense of honor among the planter elite was the cult of true womanhood, a romantic ideal characterized by purity, piety, domesticity, and submissiveness. Southern men who would protect their own honor and reputation were doubly protective of their women. Southern legend had it that a woman was faithful to her husband, a puritan in regard to morals, and the center of the Christian family. A true woman was essentially spiritual rather than physical. She occupied a separate sphere from that ambition, selfishness, and materialism that permeated the man's world of business and politics. Her place was the home, and because of her spiritual nature, she imbued her domain with piety, morality, and love. The ideal pictured her with soft, white hands that knew no work, with leisure to read romantic novels, and with a spirit of gay abandon that added life and zest to social occasions. In reality, most southern women, even planters' wives, married early and worked hard. Openly submissive to men, a true woman influenced them subtly through her purity and piety.

While romanticism in the North had many ideas that

catered to change, the South could assimilate only the most static and reactionary aspects of the movement. Southerners were particularly responsive to uninhibited sentimentality in literature, where they found escape from isolation, hard work, and the routine of plantation and farm life by entering into a romantic world of knights in shining armor. Moreover, many southerners looked upon their region as an actual reincarnation of the literary world created by Sir Walter Scott's Waverley novels that inspired tournaments, castellated architecture, a code of honor, and the enshrinement of women. These medieval romances bequeathed the most lasting monument of the Old South to the New: the fully elaborated cult of chivalry, the cult of the Lost Cause in which surviving heroes in gray became Tennysonian knights of romantic dignity and heroism, the plantation legend of graciousness and hospitality, of leisurely elegance and quaint courtliness, of pervasive kindliness and deferential courtesy. Without Scott and several southern novelists indebted to him, history would hardly have become so widespread a subject of popular interest in the South as it did in the nineteenth century. When the Enlightenment values of harmony, order, balance, and restraint collapsed as an explanatory system, romanticism, which made room for the wanderer, the alienated, and the untraditional, naturally appealed to a generation who felt the immediate past unnourishing, the present unreliable, and the future unpredictable. And southern literature was full of outsiders—of orphans, Hamlets, Hotspurs—because it was written by parvenus, the migrant, the odd: John Pendleton Kennedy, the son of Irish immigrants; William Gilmore Simms, the half-orphan; George Frederick Holmes, the wandering Englishman; William Alexander Caruthers, the failed doctor; Thomas Holley Chivers, the disgruntled; Richard Henry Wilde, the expatriate; Henry Timrod, the invalid; James Henry Hammond, the proud diffident; Hugh Swinton Legaré, the disappointed; and Edgar Allan Poe, the ecstatic rationalist. They are not a happy crew on the whole, and the predominant theme of antebellum southern romanticism is melancholy.

The Growth of Southern Nationalism

The decade before 1830 marked the beginning of what has been called a southern nationalism, a growing consciousness of regional pride. The concern for sectional advantage was evident in the reaction to proposals to admit new states to the Union in 1820–21; Maine and Missouri found opponents to their admission in the opposite region. But the crucial phase in the development of sectionalism was the passage of an objectionable tariff which precipitated the nullification controversy in South Carolina between 1828 and 1833, a struggle between Nullifiers and Unionists in the state to weigh their economic and political futures within the federal system. A nationalistic Congress had adopted tariff laws to promote a nationally self-sufficient economy and internal improvement legislation to encourage a national system of transportation. The struggle was a clash between profoundly dissimilar cultures and a confrontation between economic interests of an emerging industrialism on the one hand and of plantation agriculture on the other. By 1830, the transportation system of roads and canals, while still by no means perfect, had developed sufficiently to enable internal trade to outstrip foreign trade. With it a regional division of labor had grown up, in which the South produced exports for the entire country, the Northwest supplied foodstuffs for the South and for growing urban and industrial centers in the East, and New England and the Middle States handled most of the commerce and manufacturing of the nation. The main complaint of southerners was against the exactions of northern middlemen. Suffering from a feeling of injustice and a sense of exploitation, the South was beginning to grow aware of itself as a separate, coherent, and identifiable interest, as a consistent regional entity distinct from the North. When the Congress gave thought to a peace treaty following the American Revolution, northerners and southerners quarreled over fishing rights off the coast of Newfoundland and the right to navigate and transport goods on the Mississippi River. When the Treaty of Paris was signed in 1783, New Englanders received their coveted fishing arrangements, but southerners did not obtain their right to navigate the river and to deposit goods at New Orleans. Southerners between the Appalachian Mountains and the Mississippi looked to the great stream and its tributaries as major trade and traffic routes, and not until the purchase of Louisiana in 1803 was the right resolved. But New Englanders were never enthusiastic about the South's attempts toward transportation and deposit rights and acrimonious debate occurred in Congress from time to time because of these differences of opinion. In these sectional conflicts varying economic interests were basic.

By the second decade of the nineteenth century, sectionalism was at the root of congressional debates over such matters as internal improvements, public banks, the United States Bank, and the tariff. During the 1820s, it began to spread into other, widely differing areas of activity—further encouraged, no doubt, by such unnerving events as the growth of militant abolitionism and the Nat Turner rebellion. Southerners placed a premium on the values of loyalty, courtesy, and physical courage—the accustomed virtues of simple, agricultural societies with primitive technology, in which intelligence and skills are not important to the economy. By contrast, northerners had begun to respond to the dynamic forces of industrialization, transportation, and modern technology, and to anticipate the mobile, fluid, egalitarian, highly organized, and impersonal culture of cities and machines. The southern economy, based on cotton and tobacco, shipped its produce by river and ocean to be sold in a world market, and it needed generous credit terms to operate. The northern economy of manufacture, diversified agriculture, and

grain production, shipped by turnpike or canal to domestic markets, and its mercantile interests accumulated enough capital to be wary of inflationary, cheap credit. As a result of these differences, the South, with no domestic sales to protect, opposed protective tariffs, while the North supported them. The South opposed controls on banking by a central authority, while the northern centers of capital favored such controls. These points of rivalry made for chronic friction along lines that recurred with enough regularity to harden into barriers of sectional division. The sum of these differences was so great that North and South became separate cultures and distinct civilizations. The South was becoming a beleaguered section threatened by northerners, an ever-weakening minority group isolated by geography and cursed by a semicolonial status. In the congressional debates over such matters as internal improvements, public banks, and an objectionable tariff, it became increasingly obvious that the North, with its superior financial and population resources and its close ties with the markets of Europe, was outdistancing the South—and the region responded by turning in upon itself and adopting what could perhaps best be described as a posture of belligerent defense and a rhetoric of desperation. As they became increasingly isolated, each region reacted to a distorted image of the other—the North to a southern world of lascivious and sadistic slavedrivers; the South to a northern world of cunning Yankee traders and rabid abolitionists plotting slave insurrections. These stereotypes were damaging to the spirit of union, for they caused both sides to lose sight of how much alike they were and how many national values they shared.

As these forces of repulsion between North and South came into play, the southern states were drawn closer together by their common commitment to the slave system and their majority. Southern separatism or "southern nationalism," was in 1860 about to end in the formation of the Confederate States of America—the Confederacy as a nation. "The South," the "southern states," or even "southerners" remain enigmatic terms describing a geographical and cultural region—a land of considerable variety and a federalism of cultures—that is difficult to define. In 1787, Charles Pinckney of South Carolina declared flatly, "When I say Southern, I mean Maryland, and the states to the southward of her." Others indicated that the North and South were set apart by the Susquehanna River. The vast and varied region from the Mason-Dixon Line to the Rio Grande and from the Ozarks to the Florida Keys does not constitute a unity in geography and economy, in society and politics, or in psychology and ideology. Instead, many themes permeate the South's past. But the whole area lay within what may be called the gravitational field of an agricultural economy specializing in staple crops for which plantations proved to be effective units of production and for which African-American slaves had become the most important source of labor. This did not mean that all white southerners engaged in plantation agriculture and owned slaves—indeed, only a small minority did. It did not even mean that all of the states were heavy producers of staple crops, for the cotton states were only in the lower South. But it did mean that the economy of all of these states was tied, one way or another, to a system of plantation agriculture.

The common denominator in all this was the growth of the spirit of southernism and a desire to celebrate the South as a superior region, virtually without blemish. The Mason-Dixon Line became a kind of moral demarcation between North and South. "The Creator has beautified the face of this Union with sectional features," declared the South Carolina orator William Lowndes Yancey. "He has made the North and the South; the one the region of frost, ribbed in with ice and granite; the other baring its generous bosom to the sun and ever smiling under its influence. The climate, soil, and productions of these two grand divisions of the land, have made the character of their inhabitants. Those who occupy the one are cool, calculating, enterprising, selfish, and grasping; the inhabitants of the other are ardent, brave, and magnanimous,

more disposed to give than to accumulate, to enjoy ease rather than to labour."

By 1860, southern society had arrived at the full development of a plantation-oriented, slaveholding system with conservative values, hierarchical relationships, and authoritarian controls. The "southerner" was different from other Americans, and this difference could be defined in terms of the South's feudalism, its commitment to an antique, gentlemanly way of life. As long as the North and South had remained fairly equal in economic and political power, and as long as the "peculiar institution" of slavery had been immune to serious attack, the two sections had coexisted in a reasonably harmonious way. But as time passed, the sections ceased to be evenly balanced and slavery lost its immunity. These simultaneous developments had an overpowering effect in the South, generating a feeling of being on the defensive, the psychology of a garrison under siege. Then came the terrible moment of truth—the Civil War.

The Southern Way of Life

Southerners had the sense of their own identity as a distinct people with characteristic assumptions, values, and attitudes. At the heart of southern culture was a way of life that differed from other areas of the United States in behavior as well as in attitude. When southern self-consciousness emerged, it grew out of concrete differences from the northern colonies and states in physical environment. The climate and environment affected architecture, clothing, and seemingly even the very pace of life and speech. Blessed with a beneficent land, southerners portrayed their area as a new Garden of Eden, while the stern New England Puritans, heavily tinged with Calvinism, established their City on a Hill.

At the top of the social structure was a small class of planters who dominated society through control of land, wealth, and political power. These wealthy planters owned the best farming land, and the "big house" was the tangible symbol of their power. White racism and racial fear of slave unrest gave rise to a solidarity between the wealthy planters and the subordinate yeomen farmers—the independent landowners of the Jeffersonian ideal. Southern identity was marked by a strong attachment to local communities, to the family, and to an intense religious faith that promised ultimate salvation in the next life. Southern life was dominated by the Victorian notion of the patriarchal family, centered around deference to the father and idealization of the mother, which, biblical in origin, extended in concern and caring to children, cousins, and other kin. The rural, daily monotony was broken by rituals such as visiting neighbors and relatives, attending political gatherings and camp meetings, observing the activities of county court days, participating in community militia days, and wagering on sports such as horse racing and cockfighting. These events provided entertainment and pageantry, but they also displayed the symbols of power in this society and reinforced the hierarchical social structure and the paternalistic bonds between wealthy and plain folk.

Southerners have traditionally equated manners— the appropriate, customary, or proper way of doing things—with refinement, good breeding, sophistication, and morals, so that unmannerly behavior has been viewed as immoral behavior. The ideal of the English country gentleman provided the basis for proper manners among the Tidewater elite. Between 1830 and 1860 the cult of chivalry became a major expression of southern romanticism, and the cult had significance for a formal code of proper behavior. A regional fondness for the ritual of the splendid gesture, theatrical behavior, and extravagant pageantry appeared. Southern courtship and marriage had clear expectations of correct behavior stressing male aggressiveness and female coyness, and this romanticized ideal of mannerly behavior between the sexes was reinforced in the late nineteenth century by Victorian sentimentalism and Protestant moralism.

Like the English gentry, southerners of a comparable class were fascinated by the classical age of ancient Greece and Rome. The rage for Greek revival architecture, which seized most of the western world in the first half of the nineteenth century, was especially strong in the Old South. Southern states were dotted with towns named Troy, Athens, and Rome, and children were named Lucius, Cassius, and Marcus. Not surprisingly, higher education emphasized classical studies, not the mechanical arts. In keeping with the tastes of England, portraiture rendered by southern itinerant painters was more esteemed than landscape painting; under the influence of Gilbert Stuart and Thomas Sully, a strong neoclassical portrait tradition emerged in the Upper South, while New Orleans was a major center for portrait activity by French academicians working there between 1820 and 1850.

The dominant influence upon the decorative arts along the southeastern seaboard and in many interior areas was also English. Superior cabinetmaking developed in the coastal cities of Baltimore and Annapolis, Maryland; Norfolk and Williamsburg, Virginia; Edenton, North Carolina; and Charleston, South Carolina. Through the Federal period, Baltimore remained an important source for crafted and imported goods, though later in the period rivaled by New Orleans in influence and significance as a source for manufactured goods. Southern cabinetmakers tended to favor existing English styles, notably those to be seen in the pattern books of Thomas Sheraton and George Hepplewhite, but the region's decorative arts are rich and diverse because of contributions from Moravians, Shakers, Swiss Protestants, African-Americans, and French and Caribbean immigrants. In whatever period craftsmen have been active in the South, they have generally taken contemporary concepts of aesthetics and combined them with ideas inherited from their homelands, using available materials and tools. For example, strong rural cabinetmaking traditions emerged in North Carolina and Kentucky, using native walnut, cherry, and hickory woods. An exception to the English taste was to be found later in New Orleans, which introduced the French Empire and rococo revival styles to the Lower South.

Folk life is at the heart of southern culture, and its traditions are intimately tied to the southern way of life. Southern folk life is the legacy of the working class, both black and white, who expressed themselves through ballads and blues, folk tales, and quilts, whose culture is symbolized by the dogtrot and shotgun house, a tradition distinctly different from the classical music, novels, and portraiture associated with the wealthy, whose culture is symbolized by the columned Greek revival mansion. Though separated in many areas by caste and class, southerners nonetheless established significant cultural exchanges across these lines, as formally taught writers and artists have been drawn to and inspired by folk artists and the South's oral heritage. The result has been the merging of southern folk and academic cultures from diverse backgrounds that in time produced extraordinary literary, musical, and artistic achievements in the twentieth century. Southern vernacular houses, barns, folk art, crafts, and furniture—known as material culture—have been increasingly studied over the last several decades in order to learn how these cultural expressions are influenced by and in turn define the American South.

Craftsmen learned their skills informally through apprenticeship with older members of their family or neighbors rather than from books and formal classes; their traditions were often maintained within families through father-son or mother-daughter relationships. Stoneware pottery has often been produced in southern communities by the same families for generations. Quilts are the most colorful example of southern folk crafts; using stitched bits and pieces of cloth to evoke decorative colorful images that range from literal to abstract, from biblical to community history, the quilter created controlled, intricate designs in bright primary colors. The South's folk sculptors cut limestone gravestones, carved tobacco-shop wooden Indians, and whittled walking canes and wildfowl

decoys. Basketmaking varied in pattern and material as the location and ethnic culture of the artists changed: white-oak baskets were made by whites in Appalachia, pine-needle baskets by blacks in the Georgia Sea Islands, and cane baskets by Choctaws in Mississippi. A strong sense of place, reflecting memory and enriched by imagination, influenced southern folk artists.

Despite the stereotype of the South as a land of brick buildings, wood has been the characteristic building material of vernacular architecture in the Lowland South. Plentiful supplies of timber allowed for crude post buildings employing a small number of relatively standardized parts, assembled with the simplest of mortise-and-tenon and notch joints, and cut out quickly and assembled with ease. The distinctive southern framing system, which changed little before the Civil War, was versatile enough that buildings as small as a smokehouse or as large as a mansion could be built using essentially the same approach. This vernacular building technology was carried west by southerners into the middle western and south central states, and its influence is apparent in nineteenth-century buildings as far west as California. A typical domestic complex included a kitchen, usually a building similar in size and appearance to a one-room house; a milk house or dairy for the cool storage of dairy products; and a smokehouse for the preservation of meats. Larger complexes contained a laundry, often attached to the kitchen; an office; and, in some instances, a sunken icehouse, a school, or a small storehouse. Servants and slaves lived in the work buildings or in separate houses. This fragmentation of domestic functions into a complex of small buildings was one of the most striking aspects of the southern landscape to outsiders, whose published commentaries repeatedly compared planters' residences to small villages. At the core of the complex was the house itself.

Architecturally, the Upland South can be defined as the area lying between the Ohio River on the north, the Blue Ridge and Smoky Mountains on the east, the northern portions of the Gulf states on the south, and the Ozark Mountains on the west. Much of the distinctive vernacular architecture was brought into the region by the first European colonists, who entered the uplands through the great valley that stretches from central Pennsylvania into Tennessee or who crossed the Blue Ridge and Smoky Mountains from the east. Their architecture included log construction as well as plans derived from English and Scotch-Irish traditions and Germanic architectural designs. Popular building types and technologies began in the early nineteenth century through new migrants, popular publications, and in rare cases the direct importation of building parts and materials. The best-known building technology of the Upland South was log construction of horizontal courses locked or notched together at the corners. Framing, using pit-sawn and water-mill-sawn materials, was common for large houses throughout the nineteenth century. In those parts of the uplands where timbering was commercially practiced late in the century, steam-sawn, balloon-framed houses became common after the 1880s. Masonry construction was preferred for the largest vernacular structures since much of the Upland South contains rich stores of easily worked limestone, which was used for chimneys, foundations, and many large houses in the fertile valleys. Brick structures survive from the 1790s, but they were rare before the second decade of the nineteenth century.

Foods and diet in the South were as distinctive and varied as the building technology. As settlers reached the frontier, the pioneer family planted corn and established a herd of swine. Thus, the primary items in the diet of most southerners when the frontier had passed were cornbread and pork. Corn itself was an important vegetable. Green corn—"roasting ears"—was roasted in the shuck, boiled on the cob, or sliced off the ear and cooked in various ways. Ripe corn, treated with lye, became hominy; and hominy, dried and broken into small bits, became hominy grits. Grits cooked into a thick porridge—flavored with butter or gravy, served with sausage or ham, accompanied by bacon and eggs, baked with cheese, or sliced cold and fried in bacon grease—are so common in some parts of the South that they are routinely served for breakfast, whether asked for or not.

The food in the dining rooms of plantation mansions was far more elaborate and abundant than in the house of the ordinary southerner. Travelers and Yankee tutors have left accounts of gargantuan meals. These feasts of turtle, venison, ham, turkey, and chicken graced with fruits and vegetables in equal abundance were often accompanied with good wines, whereas in the common farmhouse whiskey was more likely to be served and drunk in tremendous quantities. Once the frontier stage had passed and predatory animals had begun to follow the Indians into oblivion, it was possible to raise poultry, and fried chicken, duck, goose, and turkey became fare for Sunday dinners and holidays. Barbecued beef and pork, usually served with cole slaw, hush puppies, and Brunswick stew, became the native fare of both black and white southerners of all economic and social strata. Country ham—the hind quarter of a hog that has been cured with salt, colored and flavored with hickory wood smoke, and hung up to age through a summer or longer—was eaten every day and at nearly every meal. In whatever form it was prepared—sliced and fried, baked or boiled—country ham is as old as the South itself. The distinctive ingredients, as well as the distinctive styles of cooking, have been common for centuries in the South. Two significant changes in food took place during the later nineteenth century. One was the growth of the great flour mills of the Middle West, which brought the price of flour down so low that even poor southerners could afford it, by which biscuits became as common as corn bread; the other was the availability of canned goods in rural areas.

Southern Architecture and Late Romantic Classicism in the Deep South

In the popular imagination, Greek revival architecture, especially the great white-columned plantation house, is symbolic of the antebellum house. In the Jacksonian age, buoyant American nationalism was crystallized in the form of templed dwellings, churches, courthouses, and capitols. The philosophical differences between North and South were not profound before 1820. Only as southerners felt compelled to defend the institution of slavery did their region become isolated and their position intransigent. The South continued to be agrarian in reality and aristocratic in aspiration; the southern mind became progressively sectional, then regionally nationalistic, and finally unilaterally expansionistic, culminating in the Confederacy and plans to annex Mexico, Cuba, and the rest of the Caribbean. One concrete manifestation of this attitude was a nationalistic architecture, a kind of fetish for white-pillared architecture in which the column became a symbol of paternalistic and chivalrous society, aristocratic rule, and hierarchical rigidity. This white-columned architecture might well have been exported, along with slavery, to any new lands the South claimed. As the North looked toward industrialization, egalitarianism, and urbanized self-sufficiency on the eve of the Civil War, the Greek revival style declined there while it remained integral to southern culture. While competing with other styles such as Gothic and Italianate, the concept of the columned-facade plantation house remained in favor in the South a decade after its demise in the North, and though acquiring a newer, more eclectic, ornamental, and aggressive vocabulary, the basic syntax was still in evidence and perhaps would have survived had the South been the victor in the Civil War. Southern culture was conservative and deeply suspicious of the Industrial Revolution; in a decentralized, agrarian economy the plantation house in the Greek-temple form was as much a symbol of stability and authority as was any seat of religion or government.

The domestic architecture of the great plantations of the Deep South was in the Greek revival style, an architecture dominated by the peripheral colonnade that was almost without exception white. The plantation house spoke eloquently for the legend of the Old South, the legend of a venerable aristocracy of noble pedigrees, seated in the stately porticoed houses or riding in supreme command over countless acres of cotton. With slaves to work the fields, the master's life was one of leisure, sustained by a firm belief in a long-standing superior culture, and born easily amid the graces of a hospitable and genteel social behavior. The Deep South, the South of the slave-owners, was the last area of Greek revival penetration. This cannot be dismissed as accidental; rather, as Vernon Parrington has said: "The pronounced drift of southern thought, in the years immediately preceding the Civil War, toward the ideal of a Greek democracy . . . was no vagrant eddy but a broadening current of tendency." As slavery became more important in southern life, the Greek revival became the best weapon in the hands of southern apologists as they moved from apology to attack, converting it from an instrument of cultural liberation into a weapon of political oppression, arriving finally at a thesis of a democracy enjoyed only by tyrants.

Into the cotton belt of the Gulf states moved a frontier society, rough, ruthless, and speculative, far removed from the chivalric aristocratic culture of legend. Nevertheless, enormous land holdings were acquired by these frontiersmen, and with these land holdings plus slave labor came financial success. Success brought cultural and social ambitions and the assumed postures of an aristocratic society. And into this promising and aggressive situation came the architectural style of romantic classicism, with all its potential for monumentality and dignified grace. Animated by ambitious dreams, modulated by an oppressive climate and traditional agrarian ways of life, and conditioned by the threads of a Palladian architectural tradition, the ancient Greek and Roman styles were re-formed into a practical and gracious idiom, the creation of a new and American architecture unique in its time and place. The Greek revival of the Deep South stood for the direct solution of practical problems. Never before in American history has so expressive a regional style taken shape so logically and quickly, or with more appropriateness to the conditions it was asked to meet. It was one of the happy coincidences of history that the emergence of a plantation society and the development of the Greek revival occurred simultaneously.

The basic character of the typical Louisiana plantation house actually had little to do with the ancient world. Its roots were rather in the Mississippi Valley, where a primitive vernacular architecture had developed while the area was still French. Because of the constant danger of flooding and perpetual dampness, the house was elevated above the ground; covered porches gave protection from the sun and provided comfortable space for outdoor living; high-ceilinged rooms with full-length windows afforded air circulation while remaining shaded by the porch. Add to the square mass the dignity and grandeur of the classical colonnade of round columns extending the full height from ground to roof and supporting the second-floor veranda at their midpoint, and the concept of the romantically classic plantation house is complete. Usually there was a simple hipped roof, sometimes with dormer windows to light the attic. By using a colossal Roman order, the two floors were unified behind the grand rhythm of the full-length columns, and the spindly posts were transformed to pillars of monumental classical dignity.

In plan, there was frequently a large central hall with magnificent rooms arranged *en suite* to allow through ventilation and handsome interior effects. The Greek revival everywhere during this period was working for greater regularity in design, greater monumentality of conception; the block plans show that in the relation between the main house and the outbuildings, which made up the whole plantation, there was an extraordinarily sure sense of studied, symmetrical, and pleasant arrangement. The great ceiling height prevalent in the Old South gave all of the rooms an atmosphere of dignity, of scale, quite different from that found in the rest of the country; the details themselves of doors, mantels, and cornices follow similar elements found in buildings of the same date almost everywhere in America as well as in the northern building handbooks. From 1830 on, the molded trims and corner blocks, the Greek profiles and mantel types became stronger, with their insistence on horizontal dignity and big scale.

By the 1840s, the nation, North and South, was firmly binding its parts together with an abundance of transportation routes. As pioneer families flooded trans-Appalachian lands swept clear of Indians during the War of 1812, steamboats and cotton brought a market revolution hard on their heels. And with federal land sales accelerating and the economy taking off both quantitatively and spatially, the West produced five new states in rapid succession—Indiana, 1816; Mississippi, 1817; Illinois, 1818; Alabama, 1819; and Missouri, 1820. During these decades, the character of American society and American life was becoming increasingly complex. The market could not gain headway along the Mississippi-Ohio river system as long as the farmer's products had to be rafted hundreds of miles down to New Orleans and the store goods laboriously rowed back upriver in keelboats. But by the end of the war, the steamboat had demonstrated upriver feasibility, and by 1820, sixty-nine of these vessels were operating on western rivers; within a decade, there were hundreds. When Paul Svinin, a Russian who visited America from 1811 to 1813, surveyed Robert Fulton's Hudson River *Paragon*, he likened it to "a whole floating town," with its dining saloon, which served one hundred fifty passengers daily, and its kitchens, where cooking was done by steam. "Gleaming silver and bronze, shining mirrors and mahogany are everywhere," he wrote, "and the most fastidious person of the most refined taste can find here everything to his liking." In order to penetrate such tributaries as far up as the Cumberland, Wabash, and Monongahela, the western steamboat's multitiered superstructure was built on a shallow raft and driven by a paddlewheel churning the surface. Western rivermen boasted that their vessels could run on a heavy dew. The three or four months required by flatboats and keelboats moving between New Orleans and Louisville was cut by steamboats to about a week. They transformed the West and cotton Southwest by carrying freight downriver and upriver for a fraction of the cost of flatboats and keelboats. Villages and towns grew up at landings as outposts of the market culture, their stores offering a tempting array of goods in exchange for the farmer's grain and livestock.

As steamboat transportation spread production for market along the river system, regional markets radiated out from the more important trading centers such as Pittsburgh, Cincinnati, and Louisville. By 1820, Cincinnati had more than nine thousand people, and in the next decade reached nearly twenty-five thousand as a meat-packing and flour-milling center. In one twelve-month period, more than four thousand steamboats put in at Cincinnati on their way up or down the Ohio River. Solid prosperity was turned into a speculative frenzy as the crosscurrents of worldwide trade, the spread of democratic ideals, new methods of production, and the steady growth of transportation and communication generated new interests and tastes that quickly reached across the land. As Europe dumped its exports on American docks at cut rates and, in turn, paid fancy prices for American staples, money-making opportunities surged across the American landscape, creating new markets everywhere. Factory-made goods were replacing the work of handicraftsmen. The furniture-making trade was still centered in the major cities of the eastern seaboard, with their orientation to Europe, particularly France and England, through pattern books. This rich reflection of international styles would be seen in the furniture imported into the Old South in coastal cities and on the Mississippi River and her tributaries. Immigrant cabinetmakers, French and German, brought with them an ethnic influence that was characterized by a range of styles of the past. It was under these circumstances from 1815 to 1840 that the classical revival style came to a climax in furniture and furnishings in what is commonly called the Empire style.

The "Grecian" style, as it was known to its contemporaries, introduced the actual use of ancient furniture forms as they were represented in the archaeological pattern books of Napoleon Bonaparte's French Empire of Percier and Fontaine and the roughly parallel versions of the English Regency. After the War of 1812, hatred of England and things English turned the attention of many to French manners and taste. The Parisian-trained *ébéniste* Charles-Honoré Lannuier of New York and the Parisian-born Anthony G. Quervelle of Philadelphia began to work in the French manner—high-style Empire pieces of mahogany and rosewood, with brass inlays, ormolu mounts, and gilt-gesso decoration—at the moment when the spiritual alliance with France was strongest. The architectural and pillared styles of the Empire and the Restoration fitted handsomely the Greek revival "temples" that were covering the American landscape. Tables were given reeded and carved, vasiform "pillar and claw" supports; sofas and pier tables in the Empire style were decorated with carved lion-paw-with-wing and dolphin feet and winged figural (swans, eagles, caryatids) or pillared supports with extensive black, gilt, and ormolu decoration. A distinctive American innovation of cabinetmakers interpreting the carved and pillared styles was the substitution of stenciled motifs and painted designs in gilt for the expensive metal mounts of early French Empire furniture. Chairs in the Greek *klismos* form, symbolic of the antique style, enjoyed a wide popularity. The furniture of the 1830s was marked by an increasing profusion of decorative detail and massive proportions. Individual assembly of furniture by independent craftsmen was being rapidly replaced by mass-production methods of interchangeable parts in factories operated with steam-powered machinery in eastern cities. With the opening of the Mississippi Valley and the Old Northwest with canals, turnpikes, and then railroads, a fast-growing population created an increasing demand for this factory-made cabinetware wherever steamboats and trains went. As early as 1830, one French-born Philadelphia cabinet-maker advertised that he was prepared to execute orders "from any part of the Union." Internal trade, multiplying twelvefold down the Mississippi to New Orleans between the 1820s and 1850s, registered a staggering growth of the specialized production and distribution of household effects by a whole new system of laborsaving machines for market in the Old South.

The World the War Made

All Americans, northern and southern, black and white, shared a common sense of having lived through violent events and unprecedented changes unleashed by the Civil War. Like a massive earthquake, the Civil War and the destruction of slavery permanently altered the landscape of southern life. The Civil War, though admittedly a tragedy and even possibly "needless," is nonetheless often described as a glorious time of gallantry, noble self-sacrifice, and high idealism. What was real and fundamental was the nobility of the two high-minded contending forces: the Yankees struggling to save the Union, dying to make men free; the Confederates fighting for great constitutional principles, such as states' rights, and defending their homes from invasion. The Civil War also had its seamy side: the political opportunism, the graft and profiteering in the filling of war contracts, the military blundering and needless loss of lives, the horrors of army hospitals and prison camps, and the ugly depths of human nature that the war exposed. Yet, there is a supreme consensus among Civil War historians: Yankees and Confederates alike fought bravely for what they believed to be just causes. Even though they have condemned the politicians of the 1850s for blundering into the war, they have written with reverence about its heroes—the martyred Abraham-like Lincoln, the Christ-like Robert E. Lee, the intrepid Stonewall Jackson, and many others in a galaxy of demigods. There were few villains in the drama. The Civil War won its place in the hearts of the American people because northerners were willing to concede that southerners had fought bravely for a cause they believed to be just; whereas southerners, with few exceptions, were willing to concede that the preservation of the Federal Union was essential to the future power of the American people.

But after 1865, when the white South accepted the reality of military defeat and when the task was, in Lincoln's words, "to bind up the nation's wounds" and "to do all which may achieve and cherish a just and lasting peace," there followed the sordid period of Radical Reconstruction (1867–77), presided over by unscrupulous "carpetbaggers" from the North, unprincipled southern white "scalawags," and ignorant freedmen. The epoch of Reconstruction has been portrayed in both history and legend as the ultimate shame of the American people; various historians have called this phase of American history "The Tragic Era," "The Dreadful Decade," "The Age of Hate," and "The Blackout of Honest Government." All told, Reconstruction was, according to this traditional interpretation, the darkest page in the saga of American history.

Recently, a sweeping reassessment of southern Reconstruction by historians has offered more sympathetic accounts of the once-despised freedmen, southern white Republicans, and northern policymakers. They recognize the shabby aspects of this era: the corruption was real, the failures obvious, the tragedy undeniable. But these revisionists have refuted the traditional description of the period as a "tragic era" of rampant misgovernment and vindictive bigotry, pointing out that Reconstruction was a time of extraordinary social and political progress for blacks, a time that witnessed the establishment of public school systems and the sincere effort to revitalize the devastated southern economy—these were commendable achievements. Reconstruction represented more than "the blackout of honest government." The peculations of some of the southern Reconstruction state governments are sordid facts, but the corruption paled before the scandals of the Grant administration—the Tweed Ring, Crédit Mobilier scandal, and Whiskey Rings in the post–Civil War North. But among the self-serving politicians and irresponsible entrepreneurs there were humanitarians who organized Freedmen's Aid Societies to help millions of southern Negroes make the difficult transition from slavery to freedom, and missionaries and teachers who went into the South on slender budgets to build churches and schools for the freedmen. Under their auspices, the Negroes first began to learn the obligations of freedom and the responsibilities for citizenship. Radical idealism was in part responsible for two of the most monumental enactments of the Reconstruction years: the Fourteenth Amendment to the Federal Constitution, which gave Negroes citizenship and promised them equal protection of the laws, and the Fifteenth Amendment, which gave them the right to vote.

Varieties of Southern Experience

At the conclusion of any great war, the belligerents commonly look for a miraculous dawn of unity and peace. Southerners who emerged out of the mingled stupidity and glory of the Civil War were no exception. Great forces and energies created by the war or growing out of it emphasized the general trend of unity. The postal system, the railroads, the telegraph networks, and the distribution of electric power developed or came into being following the war. Magazine and book publishers sought a continental circulation and ever-widening sales, developments that moved the country more and more in the direction of a common ideology. The proliferation of southern cities and towns in the next half century was astonishing; and though places like Charleston, Atlanta, and New Orleans retained strong local characteristics, urban culture is almost by definition national and cosmopolitan, not regional and parochial. The interlocking of brokers and bankers, of capitalists and corporation lawyers was a phase of this nationalism, so that, partly under their guidance, what has been called urban imperialism eroded the folkways of the countryside of the South and replaced neighborliness with impersonal social responsibility. A curious mark of change was the tendency of southern humor to polarize around two opposite typologies—the hayseed and the city slicker.

But though the forces of change and trends toward union and harmony were powerful, the era never really attained either political or cultural unity. The United States remained essentially what it had been—a tumultuous republic, a nation under perpetual stress and strain, dissidence and confusion arising from sectional animosities and bickering segments of the American people. The continuing hostility of the South toward the North and the lingering suspicion of the North about the South were injured but not killed by Appomattox and revived by the presence of Federal forces of occupation in the former Confederacy, in part created by a northern thirst for vengeance and in part a result of continuing southern intransigence. Radical Republicans tried to stay in power in the North by waving the bloody shirt, a banner that drove the South back upon a one-party stance. With farms and markets devastated by war, most southern farmers clung to a one-crop economy of cotton rather than diversifying and were therefore unable to achieve anything close to prosperity. The malaise was deep-seated and multifaceted. Except in Louisiana and a few pockets elsewhere in the Deep South, the old-style plantation was virtually dead by 1870.

What were some of the leading components of the southern experience in regionalism? What did they mean by the North? From the Confederate point of view, anybody who fought against the South, whether he came from Massachusetts or Pennsylvania or Ohio, was a Yankee. Upon closer examination, the North appears to have consisted of something called the East and something called the Middle West (the Old Northwest). But the East splits in two: One part (New England) is definite; the other (New York, Pennsylvania, New Jersey, and the border state Delaware) is indefinite. Perhaps the East was not so much an area as a set of beliefs or a myth or fictions about an area. The East, or the North, was what people thought it was, and the people who thought about it were southerners. To the South, the North was the haughty victor, strangely cruel in the sequel. The North was the officers and soldiers of an army of occupation enforcing a series of unacceptable governments. The North was the home of cotton thieves and carpetbaggers, of mudsills and immigrants, of shifty financiers and crafty politicians, of Radical Republicans and unconscionable rogues. The North held the gallant South of the Lost Cause in military subjugation, political bondage, and financial leading strings. But the situation was complex. The North was also that part of the country with money rather freely put to work to help the South get back on its feet, the home of skills to restore southern agriculture, and the source of generous, if occasionally mistaken, educational and medical charities. It was also, amazingly, a region not averse to encouraging southern writing and to publishing southern memoirs, biographies, histories, poetry, novels, and short stories. Northern realists reconciled themselves to a new variant of white supremacy that aided industrialism, and by 1886 gratefully accepted Henry Grady's description of a New South.

But what is the South? The South is the most controversial region in American history, an enigma to itself and a riddle to the nation. If one confines the South to the territory vaguely thought of as Dixie, it exhibits a diversity of terrain and development from the Florida Everglades to the Cumberland Plateau, from Delaware Bay to the Rio Grande; in this vast area there is an extraordinary range of climate. Apples are grown in the Shenandoah Valley, tobacco in North Carolina, oranges in Florida, and cotton in Mississippi. By the geographical South, one usually means the eleven states that made up the Confederacy; but of these, Florida was in a class by itself, Texas and Arkansas are usually classed as belonging to the Southwest, and Tennessee, which was theoretically in the Confederacy, like Kentucky, which did not secede, was split down the middle. Virginia seceded, but the western counties broke off and were admitted to the Union as West Virginia in 1863. The South spills over into Maryland and Delaware and over the Ohio River into southern Ohio, Indiana, and Illinois. The South, too, in the final analysis, may well be only a state of mind. Even if the South has many climates, what W. J. Cash in *The Mind of the South* calls a "cosmic conspiracy against reality in favor of romance" tended to blend the South into a single, legendary setting.

Cash is penetrating and eloquent: "The country is one of extravagant colors, of proliferating foliage and bloom, of flooding yellow sunlight, and, above all perhaps, of haze. Pale blue fogs hang above the valleys in the morning, the atmosphere smokes faintly at midday, and through the long slow afternoon cloudstacks tower from the horizon and the earth-heat quivers upward through the iridescent air, blurring every outline and rendering every object vague and problematical. I know that winter comes to the land. . . . I know there are days when the color and the haze are stripped away . . . but . . . the dominant mood, the mood that lingers in the memory, is one of well-nigh drunken reverie—of a hush that seems all the deeper for the faraway mourning of the hounds and the faraway crying of the doves—of such sweet and inexorable opiates as the rich odors of hot earth and pinewood and the perfume of the magnolia in bloom."

The Age of Romanticism
in the
Agrarian South

Swivel chair in the library at the Hermitage, Andrew Jackson's home in Tennessee. Upholstered with horsehair, the chair, originally owned by Jackson's secretary of the navy, Levi Woodbury, was made of wood from the frigate *Constitution*.

Library at the Hermitage. After retiring from political life in 1837, Jackson lived his eight remaining years at the Hermitage, where his library became the center of his daily activities. Every morning Jackson sat in the leather chair, a gift from Chief Justice Roger B. Taney, and opened his mail on the candle stand. A constant stream of visitors, including Martin Van Buren, Sam Houston, and James K. Polk, found its way to Jackson's library, and political careers were shaped by strategy planned in this room. The marble bust of Jackson was sent to him by the sculptor Luigi Persico; on the bookcase is a bust of Levi Woodbury, who served as secretary of the navy in the Jackson administration.

overleaf
Back parlor at the Hermitage. The furnishings belonged to the Jackson family. The center table was presented to the Jacksons by the citizens of New Orleans in gratitude to the general for saving their city from the British in 1815. The mantel is of Tennessee marble. The portraits in this room are often called "General Jackson's military family," as they are of officers who served with him during the Creek Wars and the War of 1812. The pianoforte was purchased by Jackson in 1839 for his granddaughter, Little Rachel, who was then seven years old.

opposite
Little Rachel's Room at the Hermitage. On November 1, 1832, Sarah and Andrew Jackson, Jr.'s first child was born at the Hermitage and was named Rachel at the request of her grandfather. On January 25, 1853, Rachel married Dr. John M. Lawrence in what was described at the time as "one of the grandest affairs ever witnessed in this part of the country." The wallpaper in this room used by Little Rachel as a girl is original, and the quilt on the bed was made by her with pieces of silk and velvet in an "exchange" with friends. In the portrait, Rachel, at eighty years of age, is shown wearing the miniature of her grandmother and namesake. Rachel Jackson Lawrence had nine children and lived to be ninety years old, dying on February 3, 1923.

Children's bedroom at the Hermitage. Five children were born to Sarah and Andrew Jackson, Jr., at the Hermitage. Andrew Jackson III was born on April 4, 1834, and christened at the White House in 1835; Martin Van Buren served as his godfather. In 1889, when the increasingly shabby Hermitage was being considered as a residence for veterans of the Confederate Army, the Ladies' Hermitage Association was organized for the purpose of saving Old Hickory's home from misuse or destruction.

Front parlor at the Hermitage. The double parlors were the center of entertainment at the Hermitage. After dinner, Jackson and his guests would adjourn to these two rooms, the men remaining in the front parlor to discuss politics, crops, and business, with the ladies gathering in the back parlor to sew and read aloud. Alfred, who lived all his life on the Hermitage plantation, recalled: "Many's the time I've seen General Jackson take Miss Sarah and dance up and down these floors when the parlor was full of company."

Rattle and Snap, near Columbia, Maury County, Tennessee, built in 1845 for George W. Polk, a relative of President James K. Polk. The colorful name Rattle and Snap was applied to the estate after it reputedly changed hands several times in one night in the mid-1800s during a gambling game. Rattle and Snap is a pristine example of the architecture of southern nationalism derived from the romantic Grecian of Minard Lafever's *Modern Builder's Guide* (1833). It is a monument to the agricultural boom of the 1840s and 1850s involving corn, wheat, cattle, and the breeding of horses as well as the culture of cotton and tobacco.

The architecture of Rattle and Snap is specifically expressive of the regional culture of the Upper South. The stately Greek revival style, popularized in America by such architects as Benjamin Henry Latrobe, reached a high point of white-pillared grandeur in Middle Tennessee shortly after William Strickland, a pupil of Latrobe, moved from Philadelphia to Tennessee in 1845 to build the Tennessee state capitol. At Rattle and Snap, the mass is baroque, having a strong extended axis around which reiterative forms that decrease in width and weight with their distance from the center are arranged symmetrically. The plan is Palladian in inspiration—a large central hall flanked by parlors, with stairs in a secondary hall at one side. Although the imposing columns are Corinthian, an Italianate theme—evident in the shallow pitch of the pediment and hipped roof, overly vertical proportions, and arcuated windows flanking the entrance—dominates the composition.

View out of the entrance hall of Rattle and Snap. The distinctive excellence of Tennessee's plantation architecture is probably the result, at least in part, of the willingness of its relatively small planter class to live on the land, personally managing their plantations. The mixed agricultural economy of Tennessee did not yield bonanzas of sudden wealth as liberally as did the new cotton lands of Mississippi, Texas, and Louisiana, but neither did it support the absentee ownership of large, single-crop plantations. It is tempting to find in the willingness of Tennessee planters to live on the land, among their fields and slaves, the agrarian idealism that characterized the Southern apologia both before and after the Civil War.

Sofa by John Henry Belter in the parlor at Rattle and Snap. Belter, one of many German-born craftsmen working in New York City in the nineteenth century, is renowned for his laminated and carved rococo revival rosewood parlor and bedroom suites. Although the principle of lamination was not a new one, Belter's method of steaming layers of wood in "cawls," or molds, so that they could be bent and carved into graceful shapes, created a distinctive style popular in the South. The sure touch of a master carver can be seen here in the lacy, laminated carving of the cresting rail with the extravagant use of naturalistic curving ornament of carved flowers, leaves, vines, acorns, and grapes.

Double parlor of Rattle and Snap, filled with furniture made by John Henry Belter in the rococo revival style. The most popular of all revival styles in the middle of the nineteenth century, it probably had more intrinsic quality than any of the others, for while it was a new interpretation of eighteenth-century rococo of the court of Louis XV, the nineteenth-century version still adhered to the earlier design vocabulary—the cabriole leg, curvilinear surfaces, S- and C- curves and scrolls, and shell carving. In the 1840s, design books began to appear in England that showed suites of this furniture, and the fashionable Parisian cabinetmakers of that time had already revived the Louis XV chair.

Parlor of Rattle and Snap. There were many imitators of Belter who were active in New York and other cities at the time, such as Charles A. Baudouine of New York and George Henkels of Philadelphia who infringed on Belter's patents. Some of the other important rococo revival cabinetmakers were August Jansen, the Meeks brothers, Alexander Roux, Léon Marcotte, and Gustav Herter in New York; Daniel Pabst and Gottlieb Vollmer in Philadelphia; François Seignouret and Prudent Mallard of New Orleans; and S. S. Johns of Cincinnati. Great improvements in mechanical techniques led to factory production of scrolls and other carved ornaments by machine. The rococo revival style, more than any other popular at mid-century, is characterized by the mass production and dissemination of inexpensive versions along with the production of superior examples by some of the most skilled craftsmen of the century.

Armoire or clothespress at Rattle and Snap. Ponderous and overworked in its detail, the Renaissance revival style was characterized by architectural forms, incorporating motifs such as a rounded or broken-arch pediments in combination with cartouches, sculpturesque crests and busts, applied medallions, acorn trimmings, and tapering baluster legs carved with the exuberance of the French baroque. Walnut, mahogany, and rosewood were the preferred woods. The Renaissance style was popularized for the entire nation at Grand Rapids, Michigan, where machine-made versions were turned out in enormous quantities, and where the elements of design became heavy and flattened. By mid-century, increased mechanization and the nation's expanding population had created new furniture centers in the Midwest producing furniture that was often both economical and stylish.

Bedroom suite in the Renaissance revival style at Rattle and Snap. Here the looseness of form of the 1840s has moved to a tightness and shapeliness of the 1860s and 1870s, from elaborate vine, floral and fruit motifs to more massive ponderous proportions and overworked detail. By this time, virtually every historic period was called upon for inspiration, and many different design sources would be incorporated into a single piece. Novelty was the keynote, and designers vied with one another to produce elaborate and showy pieces. The pediment of the bed, with its arched cresting and carved cartouche, has its source in sixteenth-century Renaissance furniture. The *meridienne* in front of the window was another innovation of the nineteenth century.

opposite

Bedroom suite in the rococo revival style at Rattle and Snap. Although furniture of the Victorian rococo, either carved or laminated and carved, was produced by many craftsmen, it has been particularly associated with John Henry Belter. The sinuous shape of the bed illustrates the importance of lamination and bending, techniques not original to Belter, but which he perfected for the sake of strength, pliability, and lightness. "Arabasket" was Belter's term for ornate and pierced rosewood furniture in the rococo revival style of the 1850s. The word is obviously a combination of arabesque and basket, with its connotation of curving lines in the shape of cornucopias and naturalistic flowers and fruit, and arabasket seems appropriate when the central bouquet is in fact in a basket.

The Green-Meldrim House, Savannah, Georgia, built by Charles Green, a wealthy cotton merchant, in 1856 and designed by John S. Norris of New York. It was largely constructed of imported materials at a cost of $93,000, which probably made it the most expensive house in Georgia at the time. Architecturally, the Green-Meldrim House is important for two reasons: it is a rare surviving example of an elaborate mid-century Gothic revival mansion in an urban setting, and its extensive verandas and entrance portico are of cast iron. The house is a conventional rectangular block, and all exterior details are Gothic. The deep bay window above the portico is crenelated and has tall, slim perpendicular lights with finely scaled tracery; the other windows on the entrance facade, which are symmetrically disposed, are square headed with Gothic hood moldings.

Drawing room of the Green-Meldrim House. The ornamental lavishness of the stucco decoration of the interior of the house seems to have little to do with the restraint of the exterior. The flamboyant detailing in the drawing room is quasi-Gothic in form but incorporates an eclectic mix of baroque and rococo elements.

overleaf

Entrance hall and doorway of the Green-Meldrim House, with a view of St. John's Episcopal Church across the way. The strong individuality of this house is typical of all domestic architecture of the Gothic revival. The Gothic designs varied, sometimes dramatically, from region to region, and there were differences even within particular regions, in the special touches of the individual patron, designer, and builder.

Drawing room of the Green-Meldrim House. In an era before the profession of interior design as we know it, there were several different options a client could pursue when setting out to decorate a house. Pattern books were the main source of advice; another important resource was the newly created department store. The most traditional approach to house decoration for those wealthy enough to be building a Gothic villa on the scale of the Green-Meldrim House was to hire a series of contractors, often under the supervision of an upholsterer, to complete the interiors.

Court Square Fountain, Montgomery, Alabama. The cast-iron fountain was ordered by the city aldermen attending the international exhibition held in St. Louis in 1904. The three-story commercial building behind the square is the antebellum Central Bank of Alabama, designed and built by the Philadelphia architect Stephen Decatur Button in the 1850s with cast-iron panels applied against the narrow elevation.

Ordeman House, in Old Alabama Town of Montgomery, Alabama, built in 1848. This Italianate town house, a typical Alabama half house with a hall to one side and double parlors to the other, was built by Charles C. Ordeman, a German immigrant who participated in architectural endeavors and entrepreneurial ventures in Montgomery during the 1850s. Behind, through the trees, is a two-story original kitchen and slave quarters building adjacent to a row of period outbuildings that served as a laundry, a necessary, and a storage building. Since 1967, Ordeman House has been operated as a house museum by the Landmarks Foundation of Montgomery.

Parlor of the Murphy House, Montgomery, Alabama. The dominant taste of mid-century America was the rococo of Louis Philippe, sometimes called "French modern" because it was the latest style, sometimes called "French antique" because it was a regeneration of the eighteenth-century cabriole leg, C- and S- scroll, and naturalistic carving of the Louis XV styles. Distinct from but subsequently merging into this revival was the regeneration of Louis XVI neoclassical furniture made by the New York firm of the French immigrant Léon Marcotte. Generally finished in black and gilt, the ebonized maple and fruitwood chairs and sofas have turned, fluted legs, square and oval molded backs, and bright ormolu appliqués. "Very rich suites of Black Wood and Gilt, covered in Moire Antique," proclaimed Marcotte's advertisement in the *New-York Evening Post* of 1860.

Gaineswood, Demopolis, Alabama, built by Nathan Bryan Whitfield between 1843 and 1861. Whitfield, a native of Lenoir County, North Carolina, bought land in Demopolis from George S. Gaines and moved his family into the log house on the property. He envisioned an estate that would represent in every way the zenith of artistic achievement. He set up carpentry and plaster shops and used machines of his own design to create his own grand estate of Greek revival architecture, for which he acted as his own architect, engineer, and builder.

Detail of architectural ornament and a stained-glass window from Gaineswood. Stained glass became extraordinarily popular after mid-century, and the Gothic revival brought it back to the attention of designers, who exploited its possibilities for rich color and flat pattern. In 1884, an Englishman, writing in *American Architect and Building News*, could say, "It is a rare occurrence to find a new building or house of any pretension without some specimen of stained, painted, or enameled glass."

opposite

Dining room of Gaineswood. Most of the furnishings in this room are original to the house. The silver epergne on the table was made especially for the room. The first permanent residents of Demopolis arrived as a result of the defeat of Napoleon at Waterloo in 1815. A large number of his exiled followers found their way to Philadelphia, where they proclaimed no other purpose than the peaceful cultivation of vineyards and olive groves; they secured from the United States government a hundred thousand acres near the confluence of the Tombigbee and Black Warrior rivers and, arriving in 1817, christened the place Demopolis—Greek for "city of people." Despite their foolhardy experiment with the cultivation of grapes and olives, Demopolis developed by 1830 into a community that was fairly typical of towns in the black belt counties of Alabama, where the economy was based on cotton and slavery. It was the ambitious and enterprising pioneers from Virginia and the Carolinas, like Nathan Bryan Whitfield who between 1817 and 1850 gave the town its first prosperity.

Parlor of Gaineswood. The elaborate plaster ceiling is identical to that in the dining room. In spite of the rigid classical nature of the architecture of Gaineswood, romantic attitudes are so pervasive that the austere neoclassicism of the house should be grouped under the term romantic classicism. During the Greek revival, the association of the American political system with the democracy of ancient Greece was inspired by sentiment as much as by reason. The late Greek revival was, indeed, a romantic movement; adopted by the common man as well as the professional, it became the first style in American history to be consciously understood and embraced as a truly national mode of building.

Drawing room at Gaineswood, Demopolis, Alabama. The mirrored recess behind the Corinthian columns is duplicated on the opposite side of the room. The matching Italian marble mantels were purchased in Philadelphia in 1853 by Whitfield's son Bryan while he was attending medical school in that city. Except for the center table and the base of the statue of Ceres, all the furnishings shown are original to the room. Across America at this time there were craftsmen producing furniture in the rococo revival style, some pieces carefully created by hand and others machine-made and clumsy. The universal chair form was the side chair with the "balloon back" produced in enormous quantities in every part of the land; another popular variant of the shape was found in chairs like these with upholstered backs.

The gardens of Rosedown, near St. Francisville, Feliciana country of Louisiana. Rosedown was built by Daniel Trumbull in 1834–35. Along the faded paths and bypaths of the gardens are all sorts of pleasant surprises—niches, footbridges, trellises, and arbors—and formal statues representing the seasons and the continents. Besides the live oaks and pecans that form the planting, there are junipers, azaleas, japonicas, bays, lavenders, and all sorts of tropical plants. Beyond the flower gardens and orchards is a playhouse and schoolroom where the children were once tutored by John James Audubon; it is no wonder, therefore, that the library of Rosedown contains an elephant folio edition of *The Birds of America*. It was there that Audubon composed a lyrical tribute to the Feliciana country of Louisiana: "It is where Nature seems to have paused, as she passed over the Earth, and opening her stores, to have strewed with unsparing hand the diversified seeds from which have sprung all the beautiful and splendid forms which I should in vain attempt to describe."

Parlor at Rosedown. The walnut sofa is thought to have been made by Prudent Mallard of New Orleans about 1850. In Victorian America, the emphasis was on the home as the central unit of society—the home was the crown of a man's life work, the fruit of his endeavor, and the symbol of his position in the community.

Bedroom at Rosedown. In the post–Civil War years, furniture achieved a massive solidity. "We have been making our furniture so heavy of late," wrote Clarence Cook in the 1870s, "that the amount of solid wood in it added to the carving, inlaying, and veneering with different woods has made it very expensive." This mahogany bed, with its monumental crested pediment and huge proportions, is an impressive reminder of what Cook had in mind.

A monumental Gothic revival bed in the principal bedroom at Rosedown. According to family tradition, this suite of furniture, made by the firm of Crawford Riddell, a Philadelphia cabinetmaker, had been intended for the White House if Henry Clay had been elected president in 1844. The Gothic revival style in furniture was marked by the distinctive characteristic of soaring verticality of the upward thrust of clustered shafts or columns and pointed arches with pendants below and quatrefoil tracery.

Dining room at Nottoway plantation, near White
Castle on the Mississippi River, Louisiana, built for
John Hampden Randolph between 1857 and 1859.
The Greek revival interior plasterwork of luxuriant
foliate motifs is symbolic of a wide variety of
subtropical plants and flowers that blossomed in the
garden. The mahogany dining-room table may have
been made in New Orleans about 1850.

Shadows-on-the-Teche, near New Iberia, Louisiana, built between 1825 and 1834 by David and Mary Clara Weeks. View from the dining room through the rear loggia over the lawn to Bayou Teche and a more recent garden house. The house has a deep porch, and in the tradition of the Caribbean and the Gulf crescent, it has no halls; instead, rooms are linked together in a shallow line, with windows and doors placed to allow for cross ventilation in the fierce Louisiana climate. Ample galleries provided open-air sitting rooms. With its tall Tuscan columns across the front, Shadows is wholly Anglo-American in its woodwork and other detailing for a plantation house found in Cajun Louisiana.

opposite
Parlor of Shadows-on-the-Teche. Shadows was a sugar plantation that hugged the banks of the Teche as it wound its way through a semitropical landscape dense in foliage, distinguished by great oak trees and Spanish moss. The house was probably completed by 1834, when David Weeks went East for medical treatment; word of his death in New Haven preceded the arrival of crates of furniture he had bought for the new house. Before he died, Mary Clara Weeks wrote her husband: "Our old furniture distributed about the rooms looks better than you would think—we have got from New Orleans one dozen thirteen-dollar chairs that I have put in the dining room."

Bedroom of Shadows-on-the-Teche. Following her husband's death, Mary Clara Weeks stayed on at Shadows as her heirs would do. Shrewd in business, she was wary of unscrupulous overseers of sugar factories and bankers. Distrustful of her French-speaking neighbors, she pulled her family close around her, children and blacks, and braced against the world. She employed a tutor, a Yale graduate named Hiram Stetson, and the six children learned their lessons at home. During the Civil War, Shadows was seized and occupied by Union troops. According to an eyewitness, its elderly mistress, "a lady . . . accustomed not only to conveniences but the elegancies of life, was driven . . . to the upstairs apartments where . . . she died—imprisoned in her own dwelling, deprived of the comforts she would have bestowed upon the humblest of her servants . . . ."

Drawing room of Melrose, Natchez, Mississippi, designed by Jacob Byers and built for John T. McMurran in 1845. The sliding doors are framed by fluted Ionic columns; a graceful plaster rosette decorates the ceiling. The McMurrans furnished Melrose with mid-nineteenth-century rococo revival furniture, probably bought in Philadelphia or New York City; they ordered the oil-burning chandelier from Cornelius and Company of Philadelphia, and it is dated 1845. The draperies, the tiebacks, and the cornices are all original to the room. When the English journalist James Stuart visited Natchez in 1830, he noted the "many handsome houses" and the "delightful views," and extolled Natchez as "one of the most beautiful towns in the United States."

Facade and octagonal entrance hall *(opposite)* of Waverley, on the west bank of the Tombigbee River, near Columbus, Mississippi; built by George H. Young in 1858. The broad and lofty rotunda soars up fifty-two feet to the cupola and measures thirty-five feet across. Young, who had migrated to Mississippi from Georgia about thirty years earlier, became a large landowner with some five hundred slaves. When he built Waverley in the late 1850s, octagonal houses were a fad; in 1848, Orson Fowler published *A Home for All*, in which he extolled the superiority of the octagonal form over the rectangular. The octagon, Fowler said, is close to the sphere, which is the more perfect shape devised by nature herself. Fowler's messianic prose style brought forth a wave of octagonal houses in the North, but only rare examples in the South. Here, Young and his architect placed the octagon within the house, creating soaring visual effects worthy of a church. The rotunda and balconies created an impressive stage set for balls and dinner parties of plantation life in the Old South.

Parlor of Waverley, near Columbus, Mississippi. Young, after practicing law, devoted himself to cotton planting with great success—eventually he owned about fifty thousand acres, and his plantations included orchards, sawmills, gristmills, warehouses, and a store. The decoration of his house varies in taste from French to Egyptian revival styles.

Bed, marble-top dresser, and armoire in a bedroom at Waverley. This set of rosewood furniture produced *en suite* was made about 1850 by Elijah Galusha of Troy, New York, who had once worked for John Henry Belter. The curvilinear forms and rococo designs of Louis XV's reign were revived in France in the 1830s during Louis Philippe's rule as a nostalgic royal rebuttal to the Empire furniture of Napoleon's regime. This borrowing of past styles and motifs and the mingling of these time-honored ingredients into the eclectic designs of the day was the epitome of artistic conservatism. One critic was moved to remark in *Art Decoration Applied to Furniture*, published in 1878: "The nineteenth century is, without doubt, a great one in many ways . . . and it is not a little singular that in the more personal service of architecture and the kindred art of furniture design it should do nothing but revive that which has been done before." This historical revival of the romantic past, begun in the 1840s, reached its zenith during the years immediately following the Civil War.

Gothic revival bookcase in the parlor at Waverley. The chief design motifs employed in the Gothic revival were the pointed or lancet arches, clustered columns, rosettes, quatrefoil tracery of glass doors, heraldic devices, crockets, trefoils, and finials. By the middle years of the nineteenth century, certain styles had been deemed appropriate for different rooms in a house. The Louis XV rococo revival was thought correct for parlors and bedrooms, while the Gothic revival, perhaps because of its connotations of remoteness and scholarly asceticism, was considered suitable for libraries.

opposite
Renaissance revival bed in the master bedroom at Waverley made by Prudent Mallard, the New Orleans furniture maker whose monumental pieces can be found in the splendor of many antebellum mansions of the South. On these pieces a rich vocabulary of Renaissance ornament was carved and applied, wrought in exotic and native woods, by Mallard. This handsomely made half-tester bed has an architectural broken-scroll pediment surmounted by an ornamental crest. In the years before the Civil War, the observant New York diarist George Templeton Strong complained of the "tyranny of custom" that led those who had enough money to spend it on furnishings in the latest French taste.

Center bedroom on the west side of Stanton Hall, Natchez, Mississippi. The marble-topped chest of drawers of rosewood veneer on walnut is probably American of about 1850; the mahogany-veneered armchair is of about 1830–40. The rosewood and ash side chair of about 1865 once belonged to Varina Howell Davis of Natchez, the wife of Jefferson Davis, president of the Confederate States of America. The portrait of the two unidentified children is signed "V. Tucker" and dated 1876.

Mantel in the front parlor of Stanton Hall. This is one of five magnificent Carrara marble mantels carved in New York City and placed in Stanton Hall by the Natchez firm of Robert Rawes and Henry Polkinghorne, Jr. The fireplace still has its original fittings and marble hearth. On the mantel is a pair of mid-nineteenth-century bronze candelabra.

Central hall of Stanton Hall. The Greek revival elements were efficiently planned and boldly executed with extraordinary qualities of geometric simplicity and revealed structure. Among the furnishings are two of the original gaseliers, now electrified, probably made by Cornelius and Baker of Philadelphia. Stanton occupied his huge new mansion for just a few weeks before he died in January 1859; after his death, his widow, children, and grandchildren lived in the house until 1893. It was occupied from 1894 to 1901 by the Stanton College for Young Ladies, and thereafter by a number of families. In 1938 the Pilgrimage Garden Club bought Stanton Hall as its headquarters.

Front parlor of Stanton Hall, Natchez, Mississippi. Built for Frederick Stanton, an immigrant from Belfast, Ireland, Stanton Hall was constructed under the direction of Captain Thomas Rose with a large number of local craftsmen between 1850 and 1858. The immense front parlor on the east side of the house is sixteen feet high, twenty-three feet wide, and fifty feet long. The ornate bronze-finished gaseliers are original. The parlor furniture includes a set of rococo revival chairs and sofas of carved laminated, rosewood, possibly made in New York City about 1850, and a mahogany center table in the manner of John Henry Belter. The enormous mirrors in the front and back parlors were imported from France, according to the *Mississippi Free Trader* of April 5, 1858.

90

Library at Stanton Hall. In the center is an English mahogany-veneered table of 1800–1810 surrounded by four matching mahogany and beech armchairs, probably French, of the same period. The large bookcase, of mahogany and mahogany veneer on white pine, was probably made in New England, 1800–1815. In front of the window is one of a pair of English rosewood globes—terrestrial and celestial— of about 1815.

opposite
Doorway from the main hall into the library of Stanton Hall, one of thirteen first-floor doorways magnificently carved from hearty pine by John A. Saunders.

Dining room of Stanton Hall. The dining table is mahogany and mahogany veneer on ash and pine and dates from about 1830; the English chairs of 1810–1820 around it are mahogany and mahogany veneer on beech and oak. On the table are a Russian silver samovar on a Sheffield-plated salver; a Sheffield epergne and candelabra; and, at the far end, a coin silver water kettle made by Jones, Shreve, Brown and Company of Boston in the 1850s.

Front parlor of Stanton Hall. This view shows the bay at the center of the east side of the house. In the bay is an American marble-topped table of rosewood veneer on pine, 1840–50.

View from the front into the back parlor of Stanton Hall. Elaborate carved wooden moldings of Greek anthemion adorn the frame of the sliding double door and an entablature with dentils around the rest of the room. In the center is a Philadelphia tilt-top table of about 1830, with mahogany veneer on tulip poplar and maple with rosewood inlay and mahogany banding. The chairs are ebonized beech and probably French. The American piano dates from 1825 to 1840 and the rosewood music stand from the 1860s.

Tampa Bay Hotel, now the University of Tampa in Florida, built in 1891 by Henry B. Plant and designed by the New York architect John A. Wood. Born to a family of modest means in Branford, Connecticut, Plant developed and promoted the west coast and central sections of Florida, bringing the railroad to Tampa in 1884. A destination in itself for the wealthy and famous who literally arrived at its door on Henry Plant's railroad, the Tampa Hotel played an important and colorful role in the city's development.

Ballroom of the Tampa Bay Hotel. In 1878, eleven years after the death of his first wife, Plant married Margaret Loughman. The Plants circled the globe buying art treasures, decorative arts, and furnishings for his hotel. It took eighty boxcars to transport their acquisitions to Tampa.

Reading room in the Henry B. Plant Museum, in the
south wing of the Tampa Bay Hotel. The exhibition
rooms retain the form and character of the 1891
railroad hotel.

Bedroom in the Henry B. Plant Museum, furnished
with Renaissance and rococo revival style pieces.

Vizcaya, Miami, Florida, designed for James Deering by F. Burrall Hoffman, Jr., with interiors by Paul Chalfin and gardens by Diego Suarez, built between 1914 and 1916. This facade overlooks Biscayne Bay. The architect, F. Burrall Hoffman, Jr., who had worked with Carrère and Hastings, produced an ingenious design for the house with four distinct elevations, each grand enough to be considered the principal facade. Built in the style of a sixteenth-century Italian Renaissance villa, Vizcaya is almost Hadrianic in scale. It cost about as much to build as the Woolworth Building, erected in New York City about the same time. More than a thousand men, many of them craftsmen brought from Europe, were said to have been on the payroll at the peak of the construction of house and gardens.

105

Rusticated garden arch carved from native porous coral rock, called oolitic limestone at Vizcaya. The coral rock has been chiseled in a technique called vermiculation. This view is through a grotto into the secret garden of Vizcaya, inspired by that at the Villa Gamberaia near Florence. In the Renaissance tradition, this small, walled secret garden served as a private retreat from the formal gardens.

South arcade of Vizcaya, looking into the music room. In these arcades around the courtyard are the simple and sturdy arches, vaults, and columns that are the basis of Italian Renaissance architecture. The arcade floor is of old Cuban tile and quarry keystone, carefully cut to show the designs of fossil shells and coral. The courtyard was used for informal entertaining and family gatherings.

Entrance loggia of Vizcaya. The tall entrance doors and frames are said to have come from the Hôtel Beauharnais, the Paris town house of Napoleon's stepson. As in most great European houses, Vizcaya's main floor was devoted to large public rooms for entertaining, while the second and third floors were given over to private quarters for Deering and nine elaborate guest rooms and suites, each with a fanciful name such as Pantaloon, Belgioioso, Cathay, or Goyesca.

East loggia of Vizcaya, overlooking Biscayne Bay, Miami, Florida. The late-eighteenth-century cedar door (one of four), with sculpted bronze decorations and a marble surround, came from the palace in Rome of Prince Torlonia, banker to Napoleon. The Torlonia arms are carved at the top of the surround and surmounted by a seventeenth-century Italian marble bust. This vaulted room, with its dramatically patterned marble floor, is reminiscent of the eighteenth-century Roman villa of Cardinal Albani.

110

Whitehall, now the Henry Morrison Flagler Museum, Palm Beach, Florida built in 1901–02; the architects were John M. Carrère and Thomas Hastings, and the interiors were designed by Auguste Pottier and William P. Stymus. Henry Morrison Flagler, a founding partner of the Standard Oil Company and pioneer developer of Florida's East Coast, presented Whitehall to his bride, Mary Lily Kenan of North Carolina, in 1901 on the occasion of their wedding. Flagler opened luxurious railroad hotels in St. Augustine in 1888 and 1889 and was determined to help develop the east coast of Florida as an American Riviera. In 1895, the many lines making up Flagler's railroad were consolidated as the Florida East Coast Railroad Line as his crews laid tracks to a point just across Lake Worth from Palm Beach (later West Palm Beach); the twin ribbons of steel reached Miami in 1896. Finally, after seemingly insurmountable obstacles and after more than $20 million, a 156-mile extension of Flagler's railroad line reached Key West in 1912, linking it to mainland Florida. The museum was founded in 1959 by Flagler's granddaughter, Jean Flagler Matthews.

opposite
Marble stair hall of Whitehall. This stair landing between the first and second floors ascends from the huge entrance hall that suggests an atrium of a Roman villa. Many varieties of marble were used here in the floor, walls, stairs, furniture, and sculpture. The bases and capitals of the columns are bronze, as are the intricate stair railings. On the second floor are fourteen guests chambers, the master suite, and Mrs. Flagler's sitting room, decorated in styles reflecting eighteenth-century France, Colonial America, the English arts and crafts movement, and the then avant-garde Art Nouveau.

overleaf

Louis XVI salon of Whitehall. The color scheme of
dove gray woodwork accented by silver was
considered rather bold at the turn of the century.
Cupids frolic in the painted sky of the ceiling, and the
Louis XVI gilt furniture is arranged in elegant but
informal groupings. The Savonnerie carpet is
entwined with flowers. Flagler's Palm Beach
mansion—called the Taj Mahal of North America—
cost $2,500,000 to build and $1,500,000 to furnish, and
yet was completed in the amazingly brief period of
eighteen months. The ladies withdrew to this room
after dinner, leaving the men at the table with brandy
and cigars.

The Age of Energy in the Industrial North

A Changing World

THE FUTURE PRESSED HEAVILY on each American in the 1830s and 1840s. In the great transformation in American life that occurred during those decades, civilization was taking shape before his very eyes. The day of the cocked hat, monarchial governments, the spinning wheel, and the horse-drawn carriage was being pushed into the discard. In its place emerged a day of pantaloons and spittoons, the factory and steam locomotive, and the triumph of democracy. From a hierarchical republic to a class-riven democracy, from Enlightenment to Romanticism, from an Atlantic civilization to a continental empire, this was a time of decision, of massive changes leading to a better tomorrow.

By 1840, millions of Americans enjoyed an easy faith in the distinctiveness of their society in its democratization and its physical expansion. The heart of their unique America was its democracy. Since American democracy was the highest form of government, this generation believed with confidence that the United States was the ideal of the oppressed people of the world—and that meant all people beyond its boundaries. America was the shining example of a free people living under an enlightened Constitution, and anyone failing to recognize this obvious fact must either be living in besotted ignorance or belong to the outmoded monarchial forces that sought to oppress the common man. Few doubted that the future would be better than the past. Progress was in the air, and change meant improvement. Was not the steamboat better than the sailing ship, the textile machine than the hand loom, Christianity than paganism, democracy than monarchy? A young and vigorous nation could have no misgivings that the future belonged to the energetic and forward-looking. God would not permit his chosen people to go anywhere but upward and onward. But time pressed and speed was essential; an intense sense of urgency obsessed men's minds, and they worked morning, noon, and night for human betterment to free slaves, reform drunkards, and lay railroad tracks with messages that were "simple, serious, and practical." As Alexis de Tocqueville commented in the 1830s: "A man builds a house in which to spend his old age, and he sells it before the roof is on; he plants a garden, and lets it just as the trees are coming into bearing; he brings a field into tillage, and leaves other men to gather the crops."

A young nation blessed with millions of acres of virgin land and comparable amounts of other resources, with immense distances to be conquered, may be excused for giving preference to the material aspects of life. This frame of mind was obvious to every foreign visitor. The Englishman Thomas Hamilton observed in 1833 that the democratic society of America provided no leisure, no audience, no sympathy, and no encouragement for arts, letters, and learning, and that taste and enlightenment among "the younger portion of the richer classes" were markedly lower than that of their fathers' generation. "Compared with the same classes in England," he continued, "one cannot but be struck with a certain resolute and obtrusive cupidity of gain, and a laxity of principle as to the means of acquiring it." He then added: "The only restraint upon these men is the law, and he is evidently considered the most skillful in his vocation who contrives to overreach his neighbor, without incurring its penalties." Wealth was not only a very pleasant possession but also the basis of social standing in a new and amorphous nation, where other lines of demarcation were often blurred or nonexistent. Wealth was the common ideal— the prize for being smarter, more ambitious, and more diligent than a neighbor. Americans lived with the international reputation for excessive love of money and the obsessive pursuit of gain.

The acquisition of wealth was for most people the favored way to improve their standing in society. Long before the term "materialism" was applied to it, the idea accumulated a considerable literature of elaboration. Reporting that a conversation between Americans was never heard without the word "dollar" being used, Frances Trollope remarked: "Such unity of purpose, such sympathy of feeling, can, I believe, be found nowhere else except, perhaps, in an ants' nest." To Charles Dickens, it appeared that "all their cares, hopes, joys, affections, virtues, and associations seemed to be melted down into dollars." Everything spiritual and temporal was measured in money. These foreign characterizations of American life took on a less unflattering form when phrased as descriptions of American work habits, which emphasized industriousness, energy, efficiency, and zeal for the task at hand. As Michel Chevalier put it in 1839: "The American mechanic is a better workman, he loves his work more, than the European. He is *initiated* not merely in the hardships but also in the rewards of industry." Adjustment to the pace of the American work ethic was a shock for European immigrant workers. They were warned by a Scottish businessman in 1877 that they should not make the effort unless prepared "to do much more than even hard-working men do here," an adjustment that Anthony Trollope thought in 1862 "to an English workman would be intolerable." Sir Charles Lyell at mid-nineteenth century described "a country where all, whether rich or poor, were laboring from morning till night" and where "the national motto should be, 'All work and no play.'" But if wealth was the goal, once obtained, it was not hoarded: "The Americans, although highly acquisitive, are not a sordid nation. They expend their wealth freely, and where the object meets with their approbation, they are even munificent in their donations." To outsiders, the United States appeared materialistic, but no American was willing to admit that his country was in any respect the inferior of decadent Europe. In every field—the writings of Washington Irving, the paintings of Washington Allston, the sermons of Lyman Beecher—the New World was willing to match the best that the Old World had to offer.

In this nation of small farmers—not an occupation that embraced fundamental changes rapidly or in which large fortunes were easily attainable—many looked toward manufacturing, commerce, and transportation to provide the main opportunities for the wealth that would make them outstanding. And a man might try several fields in his search for fame and fortune. "An American takes up, leaves, goes back to ten occupations in his life; he is constantly changing his domicile and is continually forming new enterprises," said Tocqueville, adding, "Less than any other man in the world does he fear to compromise an acquired fortune, because he knows with what facility he can gain a new one." Americans were proud of their busy factories, whether the textile mills of Lowell, the shoe factories of Brockton, the pottery works at Trenton, or the iron mills at Richmond. While Europeans of ambition and talent might pursue careers in literature, science, and the arts, Americans, in Tocqueville's damning opinion, were "swayed by no impulse but the pursuit of wealth." The pursuit of wealth had a peculiar attraction in a democracy, since democracy ruled out distinction by title, rank, or heredity, and hence wealth was likely to be the chief or only means of gaining status and distinction in society. One critic reflected the opinion of many in concluding that in America the "word *money* seems to stand as the representative of the word '*happiness*' of other countries." So the pursuit of happiness came to mean for many in the United States the pursuit of money.

Factories meant an independence from subservience to English factories, but they also meant the demise of the old-fashioned artisan and the beginning of wage labor. Sorrow and anger filled the hearts of traditional craftsmen who had been looking forward to being masters of their own small shops someday. Now they were hard put to make their livings, for how could a hand weaver compete with a textile mill full of machinery, and how could a shoemaker compete with a shoe factory? The reaction of the skilled workers was the formation of unions in the 1830s to try to hold back the tide. The making of cloth, hats, shoes, furniture, and tools increasingly left the home, and more and more the American family filled its desires by visiting a store—whether the rich city emporium of gaslights and plate-glass windows or the cluttered general store of the country. The farmer needed a surplus to trade for desired store goods, so he increasingly began to specialize in a single cash crop rather than to try to be self-sufficient.

Factories meant more trade, and together they expanded towns and cities. It was a machine civilization for these up-and-coming people. There was little argument that national prosperity depended primarily upon the moving of people and goods cheaply and rapidly over the vast continent. Roads were being macadamized and canals were being constructed in amazing profusion and projected in reckless numbers. Wild-eyed enthusiasts talked of the day when a series of canals would span the country from the Atlantic to the Pacific. Steamboats jammed the wharves of coastal cities, and thinking people realized that the death knell of the sailing vessel had been sounded. Newest and most admired of the transportation improvements was the railroad. When the first dirt was thrown for the Baltimore and Ohio Railroad in 1828 by Charles Carroll of Carrollton, last surviving signer of the Declaration of Independence, railroads had come of age. Fifty thousand people lined the streets of Baltimore to cheer the event.

Vast economic changes preoccupied people's minds, but they represented only a part of the fascinating story of a changing America. Workers in two lines of scientific endeavor made notable contributions. The first was in the collection and classification of the animals, plants, and minerals of the New World. John James Audubon is still revered for his pioneer work, *Birds of America*, while a long series of western explorations and eastern geological surveys provided a vast amount of information about the nation. The second contribution was in the realm of practical inventions, for the American was ingenious. The electric dynamo in 1831, Cyrus McCormick's reaper in 1834, John Deere's steel plow in 1839, the magnetic telegraph in 1843, the sewing machine in 1846—all these and a host of other innovations set off little agricultural and industrial revolutions of their own. A flood of inventions from the Colt revolver to the Remington rifle, from the Baldwin locomotive to the Otis elevator, from Goodyear's rubber vulcanization to the collar button—manufactured products that would become household names—were being produced in quantity and gave the lie to the prediction made early in the 1840s that the patent office might as well close for lack of business. The American system specialized in interchangeable parts as experimental tinkerers cut metal into precise parts to cut costs in an expanding economy and population. Americans were ingenious in making machines that helped to make machines—drills, saws, pumps, belts, milling machines, turret lathes. It was the age of iron—iron stoves, ships, railroad bridges, buildings, and farm equipment.

The United States was also deeply and sincerely religious in this period of material growth. And the religion so central to American thought was above all Protestant, in spite of the increasing flood of Roman Catholic immigrants, particularly Irish. The wave of agnosticism, free thinking, and deism of the Revolutionary period and the early Republic had given way to a thoroughgoing and all-embracing piety that seems exaggeratedly mawkish to the modern mind. The United States was the happy hunting ground of a number of aggressively minded Protestant sects. Many of them had sought asylum in the United States, but others were indigenous, since as long as men read the Bible for themselves and were advised to follow their own consciences, there were inevitable differences of opinion. Even the peaceful Quakers argued vigorously over a split in the church, while fragments of other sects seemed continually to be coming loose. During the first third of the nineteenth century, splinter after splinter broke from the largest denominations in the name of a purer, often a more democratic faith, pitting members against one another over the interpretation of the church's simple absolutes. Then from 1837 to 1845 the major denominations simply cleaved in two from pulls North and South: the Presbyterians in 1837, the Methodists in 1844, the Baptists in 1845. Most intriguing of the new sects was the Mormon, led by Joseph Smith, Jr., with its claim to an altered Bible.

Religion was not vague and remote but of immediate and vital importance, for men felt that God watched them every second, rewarding and punishing, advising and interfering. Man searched his conscience and pored over the words of Holy Writ to make sure he was not offending a God not who only was loving but also terrible in His justice. The family Bible was read assiduously and was accepted as literally true, word for word. Christians emphatically considered themselves their brothers' keepers, with the sacred duty to convert those less knowing to proper ideas of piety and morality. A sense of urgency spurred them on, for perfection seemed very close. Tract societies flooded the country with religious literature; Sunday Schools flourished. Sunday observance groups protested vigorously the secularizing of the Sabbath, particularly the Sunday carrying of mail. The atmospheric authority of Protestantism floated above the denominations and sects as bands of Americans set out to transform their society.

The reforming impulse, backed by strong religious convictions, swept into all sorts of movements for social improvement. Attention was finally given to paupers, the deaf and dumb, orphans, the blind, the insane, prisoners, and prostitutes. No reform movement was better advertised than that for temperance, which gradually became a prohibition drive. The same logic that had long condemned state lotteries for enticing the weak-willed to gamble condemned state authorization of liquor for enticing people to drink. At its peak between 1851 and 1855, the movement inspired prohibition laws in thirteen states from Maine to Delaware and New York to Iowa, with three others hovering on the brink. And if liquor was bad, why not also tobacco, tea, coffee—indeed anything that diverted the mind from eternal truth? Sternly conscientious men and women waged crusades against tobacco, the theater, novels, and any human foible that seemed to them to waste time better spent to the glory of the Lord. Then the militant movement collapsed. In the mid-fifties, many northerners who had once supported prohibition found their alternative in a broad, diverse antislavery cause. The sharpest set of simple truths belonged to the advocates of slavery's immediate abolition, whose movement originated in 1831 with William Lloyd Garrison's trumpet call for a relentless campaign against the sin of slave holding.

Silver parcel-gilt cup by Tiffany and Company, circa 1879.

Factories and Cities

A predominantly agricultural United States contained a surprising number and variety of factories, which made everything from ships to candles, from mattresses to the new sulfur matches. Sawmills, tanneries, and gristmills flourished by the hundreds, while distilleries were only slightly less numerous than drunkards. Massachusetts had its shoes, New Jersey its silk, Rhode Island its lace, the Ohio Valley its rope, Philadelphia and New York their pianos, Delaware its Du Pont powder, Trenton its pottery, Boston its ice, and Danbury its straw and felt hats. Other industries such as firearms, woolens, iron, agricultural machinery, and leather products expanded also, but none rose so fast in the years before 1830 as the cotton textile industry, the leader in industrial expansion between 1815 and 1860. The leader in cotton textiles was the man who set up the first such factory, Francis Cabot Lowell. Merchants in the carrying trade began to look for more secure areas in which to invest their profits following the Embargo Act of 1807, which choked off sea commerce. The cotton gin had helped boost American consumption of cotton as merchants with warehouses, easy access to credit, resources to purchase raw material in large lots, and experience in merchandising turned to cotton-textile manufacture as a way of making large and steady profits. The American standard of living was rising faster in this period than that of any other nation in the world. Most Americans were pleased with the expansion of manufacturing and the increasing use of machinery. Labor was scarce, prices were rising, and goods were in great demand.

Growing factories forecast the decline of home manufacturing, which had been characteristic of previous generations. In short, the enterprisers—the go-getters, the boosters—were taking over. Printed factory cloth seemed much more exciting than drab homespun. The result was less work for mother and more for father, who had to provide the necessary cash. The farmer was increasingly interested in crops that gave him dollars and less concerned with self-sufficiency. The resulting specialization increased average income but also increased mutual interdependence, so that economic depressions became more severe. Yet by European and especially British standards, America remained a backward country. The manufacturing industry rested mostly in the hands of individual craftsmen applying their specialized skills in their own tiny shops, most of them using tools and materials that would have been familiar to their medieval ancestors.

Manufacturing in the United States developed along such distinct lines in the first half of the nineteenth century that English observers in the 1850s referred to an "American system" of manufactures. Eli Whitney was a promoter rather than a pioneer of machine-made interchangeable parts manufacture. It was the United States Ordnance Department that was the prime mover in bringing about machine-made interchangeable parts production of small arms. The national armory at Springfield, Massachusetts, played a major role in this process, especially in its efforts to coordinate its operations with those of the Harpers Ferry Armory and John Hall's experimental rifle factory, also at Harpers Ferry. Although these federally owned arms plants were central to its efforts, the Ordnance Department also contracted with private arms-makers. By specifying interchangeability in its contracts and by giving contractors access to techniques used in the national armories, the Ordnance Department contributed significantly to the growing sophistication of metalworking and woodworking (in the case of gunstock production) in the United States by the 1850s.

The new technology spread first to the production of a consumer durable, the Singer sewing machine. The Singer approach to manufacture was called the European method because it depended largely on skilled machinists and fitters. Singer's business continued to expand both in the United States and abroad, and by 1880 the firm's world output had reached five hundred thousand annually. Cyrus McCormick adopted the manufacturing techniques developed in New England armories when he established the McCormick Reaper Works in Chicago in 1848. But between 1848 and 1880, there is little evidence that the McCormick factory expanded its technical horizons to encompass the precision techniques of special gauges, jigs, and fixtures that distinguished the arms industry. Handwork and skilled machine work appear to have prevailed at the McCormick factory. Moreover, the output of reapers and mowers remained surprisingly small: only 21,600 machines were produced in 1880, compared with half a million sewing machines Singer made that year.

While the United States was still trying to find a political identity, its inventors set out to shape the distinctive American technological character. This era witnessed the brilliant work of Oliver Evans with his automatic flour mill, Jacob Perkins with his nail-making machinery, and Amos Whittemore with his automatic machine to make wire textile cards. Countless inventors mechanized the cooperage craft, and by 1850 a wide variety of barrel-making machinery was available for purchase. Americans built pin-making machinery; clock- and lock-making machinery; and knife-, axe-, and sword-making machinery. Hardly any American inventor would have disagreed with Samuel Colt that there was nothing that could not be made by machinery.

Yankee inventors were on their way to highly mechanized clock manufacture. The Connecticut Yankee, Eli Terry, as well as other New England clockmakers, set about designing and building a series of special-purpose machines to produce wooden clocks. These clockmakers also made important marketing innovations and developed extensive private markets. As the price of brass declined significantly during the early decades of the nineteenth century, brass clockmaking developed rapidly and soon surpassed wooden clockmaking in the extent of mechanization and the volume of production. Moreover, the clock industry demonstrated that mechanization of production could dramatically reduce costs and thereby increase sales. When markets seemed to sag or competition pushed too hard, clock manufacturers introduced a new model. From the beginning of wooden clock manufacture and the Yankee peddlar system through the development of the brass clock industry in the antebellum period with its large wholesale network, the production of a large number of inexpensive or cheap clocks was always accompanied by an impressive emphasis on market strategy.

Factories meant more trade, and together they expanded the towns and cities, which seemed the very acme of rush, bustle, and modernity. The city was wicked, but it was also fascinating. Rural virtues and mores began to seem old-fashioned as this century swept on. The marveling farmer and his wife gaped in astonished admiration at the hurrying crowds, omnibuses, palatial homes, glittering stores, saloons, theaters, and hotels. Here and there they could see the very latest of modern improvements—garbage collection, sewage pipes, waterworks, coal stoves, gaslights, furnaces, and indoor plumbing. The farm seemed drab, the village dull, the town stagnant. Going back home to his tallow candles, his open fireplace, and his backhouse, the farmer could regale his neighbors with marvelous tales of the almost incredible luxury that was possible in the modern world. Novelists might be cynical or sentimental about the pull of the city on the hinterland, but their theme was more often the lure of the city for the country than it was the attraction of the coun-

tryside for the jaded metropolitan.

The young nation was inordinately proud of its mushrooming cities, which showed in concentrated form the energy of the new republic. New buildings rising on every hand, crowded streets, busy stores, congested waterfronts, and the flood of immigrants and other travelers all gave visual proof of a magnificent surge of life—a surge that surely would carry the United States to a position of dominance in the coming years. After the War of 1812, the urban imperialisms of New York, Philadelphia, and Baltimore struggled with each other for control of trans-Appalachian trade as they searched and scrambled for new routes to the interior of the country. Baltimore constructed a turnpike to the eastern end of the Cumberland Road, and Pennsylvania encouraged more wagon roads from Philadelphia. And when the Erie Canal was built as a water route from the Hudson River to Lake Erie, it combined with railroads to the West and a magnificent harbor that could reputedly hold the entire ocean shipping of the world. Thus the preeminence of New York was established among American cities.

In 1800, the population of New York City was 60,000; in 1860, its population climbed to 800,000, outdistancing Philadelphia and placing it next to London and Paris in size. The *Charleston Mercury* complained that during this period Norfolk, Charleston, Savannah, and Mobile had become suburbs of New York, while New York boosters took pride in its commercial supremacy and power. Its busy wharves were lined with sailing ships that had called at such distant ports as Canton and Calcutta, and late in the 1830s by the new and exciting steamships. Equally important, Erie Canal barges and luxurious river steamboats poured goods and passengers from upstate and from the West.

New York was a city of amazing contrasts. At the foot of the island of Manhattan, the walks, shrubbery, and trees of the Battery, connected by bridge to Castle Garden, provided a pleasing contrast to the paved wastes farther north. The lower part of the city was a maze of stores, warehouses, offices, and slums. Residential areas were farther north, at Washington Square. Here and there were the more imposing homes. But the striking feature was the mix: an old warehouse might stand side by side with a mansion, a miserable tenement might be within stone's throw of a splendid building such as City Hall or Astor House. Rapid and unplanned growth mixed together the most incongruous structures. The better New York houses were made of brick, although a scattering were of stone or wood. A typical home might have a twenty-five-foot front and a forty-five-foot depth. Marble steps, a silver-plated doorknob, and green shutters lent it an attractive appearance, which might then be marred by clotheslines on the roof or the hovel next door. At the other end of the living scale were the crowded, unsanitary firetraps that congested such areas as the Five Points.

In complete contrast to New York was America's second city, Philadelphia—well planned, orderly, and quiet. Its regular streets were paved and comparatively clean, edged with poplars and paralleled by well-laid brick sidewalks. The stores, each with an awning, though not as resplendent as those of New York, were well ordered and well stocked. Most streets were lined with pleasant brick houses, each with white marble steps, an iron railing, and a brass knob; a basement that rose above sidewalk level provided not only for storage, as of coal and wood, but also space for the kitchen. Fashionable streets such as Mulberry, Chestnut, and Walnut contained the finer homes. Everything was well tended and scrupulously clean, for the widely admired city waterworks permitted the daily scrubbing of steps and sidewalks by industrious housewives. The Quaker calm, broken only by the bustle of Market Street, led many visitors to conclude that Phila-

delphia was unprogressive and stupid, "a city of mediocrity," Thomas Hamilton concluded. The charge was not fair, as any Philadelphian would have insisted. The intellectual quality of the city was high. Scientifically, Philadelphia could claim to be the most important American center, with the most learned of scientific societies. Artistically, the city was particularly proud of its public buildings, such as the Doric portico of the Second Bank of the United States and the Ionic entrance to the Bank of Pennsylvania. From the standpoint of the patriotic, it was the site of Independence Hall, even though that historic building had fallen into serious decay by mid-century. As a progressive American city, it could point with justifiable pride to its many factories, its two wooden bridges spanning the Schuylkill, the modern waterworks at Fairmount Park, and its excellent markets. In 1860, with more than half a million in population, Philadelphia was smaller than New York but larger than Berlin. In no way—except in population—was Philadelphia willing to accept second place to any other American city.

Third and most worried of American cities in 1830 was Baltimore, which agonized as she lost ground steadily in terms of population. By 1840, she had been overtaken by Boston and New Orleans. The instant success of the Erie Canal, opened in 1825, forced the citizens of the Maryland metropolis to push the project of a Chesapeake and Ohio canal, to be followed by the even bolder construction of the Baltimore and Ohio Railroad, begun in 1828, in the contest to find a part-water, part-land route through the mountains. Baltimore possessed a reasonable harbor, but others were better. She had a fair claim to western business, but other cities were superior. Hence, while Baltimore attracted a moderate amount of business and a few immigrants, she found herself continually slipping in the race for commercial dominance. The Baltimoreans could and did take great pride in the attractiveness of their streets, of their monuments, of their public buildings; the Catholic cathedral was unusually impressive, for this was the greatest American center of Catholicism.

The one great urban center of New England was Boston, with some hundred thousand residents in 1840. Bostonians were not unduly modest concerning the city's virtues; one presumably disgruntled commentator wrote sarcastically that "many people, especially Bostonians, find it the finest city in the United States." New Englanders were the most stereotyped of all Americans, and the usual portrait was not favorable. Thomas Hamilton concluded: "One meets in them much to approve, little to admire, and nothing to love. . . . Nature, in framing a Yankee, seems to have given him double brains, and half heart." The Yankee appeared most frequently to the rest of the country as a solemn and sanctimonious hustler, frequently a peripatetic peddlar who from the pack on his back sold all kinds of gimcracks, including clocks that would not run, wooden nutmegs, and sanded sugar. His reputation included credit for being the sharpest trader on the continent. This calm assumption of outstanding excellence infuriated many visitors, and even irritated other New Englanders who looked to Boston for leadership. One New Hampshire resident remarked bitterly: "It seems as though your Bay folks thought all sense and knowledge belonged to them."

No matter how irritated the visitor, he had to admit that Boston was an attractive city with its many prosperous-looking granite and brick buildings and its universal white Venetian blinds. While the streets were narrow and winding, they were comparatively clean. The town centered on the Common, which was enclosed by a handsome iron fence and edged by some of the finer residences of the city; Beacon Hill was impressive. The Boston of Ralph Waldo Emerson's boyhood, where he played in gardens on Summer and Chauncy streets and where he had driven his mother's cow to pasture along Beacon Street, had been a pleasant mixture of city and country. But Boston's air changed considerably in Emerson's own lifetime. In the early 1830s the railroad invaded the city with the opening of lines to Lowell, Providence, and Worcester; and at the same time the spacious Beacon Hill mansion of Gardiner Greene was sold to land speculators. In 1834 Emerson finally moved to Concord at a time when he felt that a country environment was the most compelling need of his spirit. He wrote to his friend Thomas Carlyle in 1840: "I always seem to suffer some loss of faith on entering cities. They are great conspiracies; the parties are all maskers, who have taken mutual oaths of silence not to betray each other's secret and each to keep the other's madness in countenance."

Boston's main business thoroughfare, Washington Street, was lined with clean and well-stocked stores. The harbor was crowded with ships, up to five hundred at a time. Impossible for the visitor to miss was the new Tremont House on Beacon Street—a pretentious three-story hostelry made impressive by its portico and fluted columns, and containing one hundred eighty elegant rooms replete with the latest conveniences. Other sources of Bostonian pride included the Boston Athenaeum Library, Massachusetts General Hospital, and Bunker Hill Monument. A visitor was encouraged to attend one of three theaters or to worship at one of fifty churches.

The political capital of the nation was a young dream city—described by Ernest Samuels, Henry Adams's biographer, as a "city built on the edge of a swamp, a sort of parody of the American dream"—with vast aspirations expressed by magnificent distances, but marked more obviously and immediately by a straggling of brick and frame houses and taverns, and bottomless streets. "Everybody knows that Washington has a Capitol; but the misfortune is that the Capitol wants a city," Captain

Frederick Marryat wryly commented in 1839. "There it stands, reminding you of a general without an army, only surrounded and followed by a parcel of ragged, dirty little boys; for such is the appearance of the dirty, straggling, ill-built houses which lie at the foot of it." Many people felt that the tone of society corresponded to the city's physical appearance. "It is the City of Selfishness. It is a den of thieves," wrote Samuel Gridley Howe, adding, "It is the place where wicked men most do congregate, and it is the more intolerable because they are generally the ablest rogues in the country."

Adverse criticisms of Washington were not universal. Many people thought the city a pleasant place, insisting that the architecture was impressive and that unfinished buildings spread over vast distances merely presaged a magnificent tomorrow. True, most of the streets were impassable much of the time, but they were all wide, and Pennsylvania Avenue was paved. More important, the city's advocates pointed out that the society was interestingly mixed, while the foreign legations gave a touch of the exotic. In 1877, Henry Adams moved to Washington from Boston and began his forty years' residence there. "Home was Washington," he exclaimed with pleasure. "This is the only place in America where society amuses me or where life offers variety."

In time, the eastern seaboard became beaded with towns, many of them so well situated with respect to geographic and trading advantages as to grow into the great cities of today. The establishment of settlements like Albany, New York, and Lancaster, Pennsylvania, moreover foreshadowed the rise of urban communities inland. Buffalo and Pittsburgh, on the border between East and West, had unusual promise for the future. Younger of the two, hence cruder and more boisterous, was Buffalo; no more than a village in 1830, it swelled to a population of 20,000 within the next decade. Buffalo was a boomtown, astride the junction of the Erie Canal with Lake Erie; with land speculation ever present, its prosperity seemed assured for all time. Along the wide streets new buildings seemed to rise overnight. Big, ramshackle, wooden hotels were so crowded that men bedded in the halls and women slept five or six to a room. The streets were jammed with not only local residents but immigrants, land speculators, fugitives to and from Canada, runaway slaves and their pursuing masters, Indians, and merchants.

Pittsburgh considered itself the "gateway to the West" and was buttressing its claim with an elaborate system of canals, inclined planes, and railroads to the East. It was daily being transformed into the "Birmingham of America" as it developed its manufacturing of iron, glass, ships, engines, liquor, and other products. The official population of slightly less than 20,000 in 1830 seemed a gross underenumeration as men rushed in the staccato emphasis of business. Pittsburgh citizens seemed in a perpetual hurry. It was an extremely attractive city for the businessman in search of profits, but it was extraordinarily unpleasant for the traveler looking for beauty and comfort. The city was compact and dirty; the streets were badly paved and the houses dingy. No traveler failed to note the "voluminous column of smoke, which mounted slowly, but majestically, into the regions of attenuated air."

Meanwhile, farther downstream on the Ohio River, Cincinnati boasted a meat-packing business that won it the sobriquet of Porkopolis; but by 1890, with a population of a quarter million people and hosting an accomplished music academy and nourishing distinguished artists and writers, Cincinnati became known as "the Paris of America."

Hundreds of other smaller American cities either flourished or wasted away. Some were old and some were new, but each boasted proudly of its public buildings, comfortable houses, promising industries, and potential roads, canals, and railroads. Each was inhabited by optimistic Americans who looked to the future with confidence—a confidence that was not always justified. Whatever American failings were, living in the past was not one of them.

Gothic revival chair designed by Alexander J. Davis.

The Gilded Age

American democratic culture—despite the terrible record of wartime casualties, the mingled stupidity and glory of the holocaust, and the long shadow of a murdered president—survived the Civil War to dominate the balance of the nineteenth century. These were complex, formative years, and no single story or historical paradigm can impose unity on all the themes of America's transition from a new nation, bearing a revolutionary legacy, to a modern nation, trying to chart a course down the stream of time. The Industrial Revolution and the development of commercial monopolies, Reconstruction and the New South, massive immigration and the heyday of the robber barons, the settlement of the West and closing of the frontier—all brought to the fore of public life a cast of characters that was very different from the statesmen, soldiers, and slaves of the Civil War. We came out of the Civil War a great military and economic power, strong, unpredictable, and parochial. We turned our gaze inward under a succession of presidents who were at the best high-class mediocrities and at the worst Ulysses S. Grant. We became industrialized. We undertook, and were almost wrecked on, a series of fatuous policies for the postbellum South. We passed in literature from the standard classical American authors to another set of writers who had been "Europeanized"; we produced a large number of painters and architects whose work was also Europeanized. We patronized American composers mainly educated in Europe. Toward the close of the century, our scientists and philosophers achieved a modest equality with Europe.

The West was settled at a fatal cost to the North American Indian. The South was tied back to the Union at a humiliating cost to the American black. We walked through the valley of humiliation in the panic of 1873 and the depression of 1893, each having devastating effects on the economy. The splendors of the new cities rose amid the squalor of industrial slums. Our municipal governments were the worst in the world; the amazing industrial expansion of the United States was accomplished with considerable exploitation of factory artisans. Theoretically we welcomed the poor of the world to our democratic shores, the symbol being donated by France, with an inscription on its base written by a Sephardic Jewess named Emma Lazarus. Practically, however, we kept the black in his place, the Indian on his reservation, the Hispanic in his alley, and the Jew in his ghetto. The most damning indictment of this postwar American society was attributed to the future French prime minister Georges Clemenceau, who lived in America for a time. Noting its undoubted problems, he could claim the United States had gone from a stage of barbarism to one of decadence without achieving any civilization between the two. Mark Twain paid a different but no less censorious tribute to the aspirations, autocracy, and affluence of the new American plutocracy of industrialists, financiers, and politicians in his utopian satire, *The Gilded Age* (1873).

Yet during these decades, at once depressing and brilliant, America produced the most amazing gallery of powerful and picturesque personalities we have fostered in almost any age. If we gutted the land, staged some of the bloodiest labor conflicts in our industrial history, and suffered from a continual neurosis of sectionalism and paranoia about foreigners, we also gave birth to a race of dreamers and reformers the like of which we had not seen before, not even during the time of the Transcendentalists. In this half century every reformer carried a utopia in his head, every protest was against the whole establishment, every dismal prophecy predicted the coming transformation of the country by violence into a tyranny or, contrariwise, saw beyond immediate collapse a communal heaven ultimately to be reached by evolution and reform. The reform movement in the big cities was essentially a bourgeois phenomenon, rooted in middle-class fears of urban disorder, immigrant ways, and family disruption.

A powerful Jeffersonian rural myth persisted—the conviction that the city, although obviously different from the village in its external aspects, should nevertheless replicate the moral order of the village. The conflict was between the big city bosses and the lords of reform—a clash of ideologies between value systems, ethnic groups, class outlooks, and power systems. The reformers viewed the bosses as representing all they disliked in politics— corruption, manipulation, links with the underworld, and ties with monopolistic, favor-seeking businessmen. The businessman, Lincoln Steffens concluded, was the chief source of corruption. But many of the reformers were businessmen themselves and would not challenge the system of private property and corporate power that lay at the foundation of the industrial city. So ultimately, most reformers proved more interested in saving the lower class from liquor, gambling, and prostitutes—basic and necessary releases for those with few other means of diversion—than in reforming the social and economic system in which so many of the poor were trapped. There was, indeed, a dangerously antidemocratic edge in the outlook of some of these reformers in reacting against "the dangerous classes" who cared "nothing for our liberty and civilization." The curse of the city, wrote E. L. Godkin of the *Nation*, is the "people"—or the half of them that comprised the poor, "that huge body of ignorant and corrupt voters." From this vantage point, it was but a short step toward proposals to restrict the suffrage to the propertied class, to bar the poor immigrant, the unschooled, and the illiterate from the polls.

Society in the Gilded Age was indulgent of commercial speculation and social ostentation but indifferent to the special needs of immigrants and Native Americans and intolerant of black Americans, labor unions, and political dissidents. This was a period of predominantly Republican administrations led by ineffective presidents and the promise of American life thus lay in its industrial future. The Centennial Exhibition, which opened on the banks of the Schuylkill River outside Philadelphia in May 1876, emphasized America's mastery in the appliance of science. Machinery Hall was guarded by a huge breech-loading cannon, the symbol of war, and by the enormous Corliss steam engine, a new symbol of peace and progress. Between 1865 and 1901, the American Industrial Revolution transformed the United States from a country of small and isolated communities scattered across three million square miles of continental territory into a compact and industrial unit.

The United States was fabulously rich in minerals: great resources of petroleum and coal; immense deposits of high-quality iron ore; and, in the West, a natural treasury of gold, silver, and copper. Although in 1860 the United States was still a second-rate industrial power, by 1890 the value of its manufactured goods almost equaled the total of Britain, France and Germany. In the 1890s, American cities were modernized, and steel was the essential medium used for building bridges, piping water and sewage, transmitting gas and electricity, and constructing even higher buildings. Iron replaced wood; steel replaced iron; and electricity and steam replaced horsepower. Industrial growth and westward expansion were assured by the revolution in communications. Telegraph and telephone, and the press increased public knowledge and business efficiency. There was a spectacular growth in population, from 35.7 million in 1865 to 77.5 million in 1901; yet these widely dispersed people felt part of a unified whole. A transcontinental railroad network, the basis of the new industrial economy, brought farm and factory,

country and town closer together. Railroad bridging in America was a wonder of thrift, thanks mainly to the Howe truss whose wood and iron components could be mass-produced and shipped to the construction site. By their aptitude for invention and their ability to harness the inventions of others to their own purposes, Americans acquired a facility for turning raw materials into finished industrial products. As many as 440,000 patents were issued for new inventions between 1860 and 1890. During the Gilded Age, the most significant American inventions were those that could hasten and secure settlement: steam boilers, the electric lamp, the telephone, linoleum, the elevator, and the typewriter. The years were a brilliant epoch driven steadily forward by a mysterious compulsion known as progress.

According to most interpretations of the Gilded Age, sharp practice became standard practice in commerce and politics. Whereas the English historian Thomas Carlyle called the entrepreneurs of the Industrial Revolution captains of industry, they were known more commonly in America as robber barons—rogue financiers eager to make a killing, especially in railroads and public utilities. They were ruthless and aimed for monopoly control of a product or market. The Gilded Age saw the development of the modern corporation in the United States. The corporation existed as a screen for the dark doings of speculators, as a shield to hide the actual operations of competitive ruthlessness, and as a vast new device for the exploitation of power and the selling of "watered stock." These new creations, expanding both horizontally and vertically, took the nation, the continent, or the world for their empires, swelling rapidly into institutions that rivaled the government in power and energy. Corporations were damned as "trusts"; they were perceived by the rural mind as uncontrollable, soulless, evil giants who were turning an agrarian republic into an empire of greed. To the capitalist, the investor, and the business genius, the corporation was the last fine flowering of the Protestant ethic, the philosophy of rugged individualism, the inevitable product of and answer to what came to be known as Social Darwinism.

Robber barons were accountable to no one. Their control was always autocratic, their life-style frequently opulent. They flaunted their wealth in their houses and furnishings, painting the gilded lily. Godkin described the United States in 1866 as a "gaudy stream of bespangled, belaced and beruffled barbarians. . . . Who knows how to be rich in America? Plenty of people know how to get money; but . . . to be rich properly is, indeed, a fine art. It requires culture, imagination, and character." The extravagance of robber barons and politicians in their employ gave the Gilded Age much of its character. Not since the heyday of the Venetian Republic had successful merchant families indulged themselves in such ostentatious displays of wealth and vulgarity. To enrich their homes and give society notice of their new status, robber barons acquired paintings, furniture, sculptures, books, and manuscripts of great cultural value. The sophistication they could not achieve within themselves by education they could borrow or amass for themselves by possession. The absolute distinction was ownership of a unique object of art. A spirit of *noblesse oblige* pervaded the families of the robber barons, who believed that it was their duty to found such major cultural institutions as museums, universities, libraries, and opera houses.

The centennial of 1876 had not only awakened Americans to the potential of the Industrial Revolution but had also rekindled their interest in previous cultures; the displays alerted them to the origins of their culture in other nations. For many artists, architects, scholars, and cabinetmakers, there followed an American Renaissance comparable to the Italian Renaissance of the fifteenth and sixteenth centuries. It extended beyond the distin-guished paintings of John Singer Sargent, Winslow Homer, and Thomas Eakins to all the visual and decorative arts. It reached the height of achievement in the World's Columbian Exposition of 1893 on the shores of Lake Michigan in Chicago. At no time in American history has such a brilliant group of architects, designers, painters, and sculptors from all over the United States worked more harmoniously toward a common artistic goal than those enlisted in creating the Exposition—a truth attested to by Augustus Saint-Gaudens's famous assertion to a plenary session of the artists and planners: "Gentlemen, do you realize that not since the Renaissance has a comparable group been brought together for an enterprise like this?" Calling the style classical—inspired by the glory that was Greece and the grandeur that was Rome—or Beaux-Arts, or American Renaissance, a visitor to the Exposition would not soon forget this vision of an imperial country, the great offspring of Republican Rome, taking shape as a White City adorned with columns and statues, colonnades and triumphal arches, made fair with stately buildings and illuminated at night by that new wonder, the electric light.

The same heady exuberance, the same avid thirst for experience, the same desire to taste other cultures and sample other centuries created or filled the palaces of the new rich, an opulent and ostentatious plutocracy. In the houses of millionaires on Fifth Avenue in New York, on Michigan Boulevard in Chicago, at Newport, Tuxedo Park, or elsewhere, statues of bronze or alabaster, scimitars, antlers, Oriental lamps, and sculptured busts vied for attention with canvases by Old Master painters and artists of more perdurable fame. So did Herter and Marcotte furniture, French *objets d'art*, Dresden china, elaborate silver, brass bedsteads, and upholstered, tufted sofas. In the Cyrus McCormick Mansion in Chicago, with its main hall patterned after a castle of Henri IV of France, the ceiling of the dining room touchingly combined the cross of the Foreign Legion of Honor, a reaper, sheaves of grain, and the names of Pomona, Flora, Ceres, and Diana. Armsmere, Samuel Colt's house in Hartford, was basically an Italianate villa but had an Oriental dome, various attached greenhouses, and an equestrian statue in front. Frederic E. Church's Olana above Hudson, New York, was described by a contemporary art journal as "Persian in inspiration," with "shallow arches, over doors and windows . . . bordered with mosaic tiles, its minarets and spindlelike columns painted originally in bright colors," all supposed to suggest something on the Bosporus or in the Near East. The imagination flags before this procession of opulent Gilded Age structures built to demonstrate conspicuous expenditure and exhibit conspicuous waste. Following the economic doctrine that the country necessarily benefited from wealth, in the winter of 1897, the Bradley Martins determined to give a ball in order to decrease national unemployment during that panic year. It was held at the Waldorf-Astoria Hotel, and the total expenditure was said to be $369,000. The guests came dressed as Renaissance, Elizabethan, Dutch, and French historical characters. But it was the last festival of its kind. The Bradley Martins were so severely attacked by press and pulpit, anarchists and agitators, representatives of labor and social workers, that they withdrew from the United States altogether. Two years later, Thorstein Veblen published *The Theory of the Leisure Class,* in which he turned the Horatio Alger myth upside down and struck out at the most sacred of idols. The overarching theme of this work was the subordination in capitalistic America of industry to business, of the industrial arts to financial gain, of rational use to conspicuous waste, of genuine human values to money values, of function to ownership.

The public persona of the self-made man was based on a cult of outward modesty and respectability. And as a rule,

the robber barons—the lawless financiers and industrial magnates of the Gilded Age—were puritanical, parsimonious, and pious. The captains of industry usually preferred the myth that they had made their money by the sweat of their brow. In their excessive egotism, the leading business personalities of the age were aware of the curious parallelism of their values and their actions to those of the Italian mercantile princes of the Renaissance; it is instructive to remember that the palaces of Italian cities were in fact the models of some of the "cottages" built by the Vanderbilts in Newport. The egotism of Venetian merchants, who thought the world existed for their profit, precedes but does not surpass an attitude expressed by John D. Rockefeller, who claimed: "God gave me my wealth." As the robber barons accumulated wealth, like the Medici they sought to patronize culture, and like the medieval feudal lords they turned to philanthropy for the salvation of their souls. They also sought in many cases to perpetuate a personal dynasty. Their skill in economic exploitation, in creating combinations and trusts, in buying up courts and legislatures, senatorial elections, and appointments to the federal bench, in the manipulation of stock markets, the use of rebates and simulated panics, and prices artificially lowered and taxation increased to crush a competitor, must be balanced against their founding of libraries and art museums, hospitals and scientific institutes, and the creation of schools and colleges, and the beginnings of vast foundations for scholarship, scientific research, medicine, charity, and education. The difficulty in dealing with these men is to know what is fact and what is fiction. The Gilded Age produced its own legends as readily as it produced its own lives.

At the end of the nineteenth century, however, the United States retained its essential character; it was a nation under perpetual stress and strain. Although the half century moved toward nationalism and uniformity and, at the end, imperialism, those movements were continually slowed or checked by tensions among various regions and bickering elements of the American people. The obvious example was the continuing hostility of the South toward the North and the lingering suspicion of the North about the South. The age was filled with contradictions and rich confusion; at the same time, everything was flexible, everything was possible—the New South, the Great West, university reform, bimetallism, populism and progressivism, aesthetics, higher morality, greater "sophistication," "the White Man's burden," the strenuous life, art for the people, more millionaires, a more equitable distribution of the national wealth. One is tempted to quote the opening lines of *A Tale of Two Cities:* "It was the best of times, it was the worst of time, it was the age of wisdom, it was the age of foolishness, it was the season of Light, it was the season of Darkness, it was the spring of hope, it was the winter of despair."

The Age of Energy
in the
Industrial North

Victoria Mansion, built for Ruggles Sylvester Morse of New Orleans, in Portland, Maine, 1858–1860, from designs by Henry Austin of New Haven, Connecticut. Morse was born in 1816 to a shipbuilding and commercial family of Leeds, Maine. After working for the Tremont House in Boston and the Astor House in New York, he went to New Orleans where he became the manager and proprietor of the most elaborate "palace hotels" in the nation. He made a substantial fortune also as a commercial banker and principal of a wholesale drug firm. His fortune assured, he returned to Maine with his wife, the former Olive Merrill of Durham, Maine, to plan a summer house away from the heat and humidity of Louisiana. The prominent feature of the Italianate style villa is the tower which gave the Morses a commanding view of the river and the harbor. For the exterior the architect Austin chose Portland, Connecticut, brownstone with painted stuccoed brick and sanded wood, all used to look like stone.

opposite

Dining room of Victoria Mansion. Behind the reception room the French Renaissance Revival dining room boasts chestnut-paneled walls of flat and quarter-sawn oak panelled walls carved to represent fruits, vegetables, game, and fish, including the Maine lobster. The ceiling is grain-painted to look like wood. The elaborately carved chairs, dining table, and sideboard were all designed for the room.

Entrance hall of Victoria Mansion. Dominating
the impressive space, with a vertical height of
approximately forty feet, is the flying staircase
of Santo Domingo mahogany. The height of the
great two-tiered gas chandelier is eighteen feet.
The decoration of the hall is trompe l'oeil panels
en grisaille, wainscot grained to resemble rare woods,
decorative plaster ceiling enriched with applied
gold leaf and mixed-media Renaissance revival style
cartouche work, and oil paintings on canvas applied
to the walls within gold leaf bezels. Large lunette oil
paintings on canvas are attached to the cornice frieze
portraying three of the four Biblical-classical virtues:
fortitude, prudence, and justice; Columbia replaces
the missing virtue of temperance. On the landing a
stained-glass window depicts the state seals of Maine
and Louisiana. The French bronze statues were
purchased by Morse at the Robb sale in New Orleans
in 1859.

Reception room of Victoria Mansion. The room
was also called the music room and its purpose is
reflected in the dancing figures of the Carrara marble
fireplace and the many lyres and singing cherubs that
ornament the walls. The arts—painting, architecture,
music, and literature—are the subjects of paintings
that center each cornice frieze. As was the fashion of
the time, the architect Austin created eclectic
designs skillfully combining the features of many
historical styles into delightful and elaborate wholes.
Here in the reception or music room he has captured
the essence of the baroque style in its symmetrical
decoration on the walls and ceiling and the heavy
French plate glass overmantel mirror and matching
cornices. Flanking the hearth are portraits of Mr. and
Mrs. Ruggles Sylvester Morse presumed to have been
painted in New Orleans shortly before or after the
marriage of the young couple in 1852; the artist is
unknown.

Drawing room of Victoria Mansion. Primarily decorated in white and gold, the drawing room reveals all the stylish glories of the architect Austin's imagination. Gustave Herter of New York City was the interiors contractor for Morse between 1859 and 1862, making some of the furniture himself, and apparently subcontracting the other pieces of furniture, interior trim, marble, plaster, wall decoration, and textiles to various vendors; the interior wall finishes were by Giuseppe Guidicini of New York. Mirrors and French plate glass windows enhance the space of this room; cherubs and roses embellish the ceiling, cornices, and even the gas chandelier. The sofas and chairs, original to the room, epitomize the high-style Franco-European taste of the 1850s. The drawing room retains its original carpet manufactured by James Templeton & Sons of Glasgow, Scotland, its colors and design echoing the decoration of the ceiling.

Breakfast room of the Skolfield-Whittier House, Brunswick, Maine, a brick double house built between 1858 and 1860 by George Skolfield, a prominent Brunswick shipbuilder and sea captain, for his sons, Samuel and Alfred. This room from Alfred's side of the house is furnished with furniture and household objects that he and his bride, Martha Isabella Harward, purchased in late 1862. The landmark Skolfield-Whittier House is now the headquarters of the Pejepscot Historical Society.

Pantry of the Skolfield-Whittier House. The second era of the Skolfield-Whittier House was marked by the death of Alfred Skolfield in June 1895 and the marriage of his daughter Eugenie to Dr. Frank N. Whittier, Bowdoin College physician, in the same month. With the birth of three daughters, the third generation of the family and live-in baby nurses and housekeepers populated the house and made service areas like the food pantry important and necessary.

Drawing room of the Skolfield-Whittier House.

The so-called Wedding Cake House, Kennebunk, Maine. It belonged to a sea captain who made his eighteenth-century foursquare home fashionable by adding the gaudy architectural Gothic lacework. The Gothic revival in architecture was literary and sentimental in origin; no sight was more enchanting to the Victorians than a broken castle or a ruined abbey. The broken, picturesque exteriors of full-blown Gothic-style stone mansions were translated into "Carpenter Gothic" in which the stone tracery became wooden fretwork or "gingerbread" cut with a scroll saw; the exterior of these new Gothic cottages made the most of the effects of sunlight, shade, and foliage. The architectural pattern books contained only a few drawings of brackets—local carpenters and lumber mills worked out their own fanciful gingerbread designs of scrolls and curlicues, which became the universal design language of the nineteenth century.

opposite
Parlor of the Colonel John Black Mansion in Ellsworth, Maine, built between 1824 and 1828. In 1802, Black married the daughter of General David Cobb, a member of George Washington's military family and speculator in Maine lands, and built this house on a three-hundred-acre plot, a gift from his father-in-law. Bricks for the house are said to have come by sea from Philadelphia, and tradition affirms that it took skilled workmen from Boston three years to complete the work on the house. The Black House was lived in by three generations of the family; in 1928, the estate was bequeathed to the public by a grandson of John Black.

144

overleaf

Library of the Putnam-Balch House, Salem, Massachusetts, built in 1871–72 by John Silver Putnam. Putnam, a manufacturer of leather goods, lived in the house less than a year before his death in 1873; the house was then acquired in 1881 by Edward F. Balch, the agent of Salem's great Naumkeag Steam Cotton Mills. The walnut and burl-walnut Renaissance revival bookcase at the right dates from about 1875 and may have been made in New York City. A Parisian bust of Johann Christoph Friedrich von Schiller, the German poet, adorns the walnut partner's desk of about 1875. In the left corner is a mahogany Colonial revival corner cupboard of about 1880 with beveled glass doors. Above the mahogany lyre-base card table on the left, attributed to the Vose family of cabinetmakers of Boston, is a framed Tiffany window depicting Father Christmas holding the Christ Child, made in New York City about 1890.

Entrance hall of the Putnam-Balch House. The Colonial revival tall-case clock was made by J. E. Caldwell and Company of Philadelphia. Opposite it is a rococo revival étagère of about 1870 used for the display of porcelain.

Dining room of the Putnam-Balch House. The decorative elements of the house reflect the seemingly limitless potential of machine-made ornament in the years immediately following the Civil War, and show a combination of French academic (Second Empire) and high Victorian Italianate styles. The ponderous Renaissance revival sideboard was made about 1875 by Herter Brothers in New York City. The mahogany dining-room table of about 1850 is twenty-two feet long and surrounded by eight Victorian rosewood side chairs.

Drawing room of the Putnam-Balch House.

Principal bedroom of the Putnam-Balch House. The rococo revival rosewood tall-post bed is attributed to Prudent Mallard of New Orleans and dates from about 1850. The Colonial revival upholstered lolling chair, c. 1850, is modeled after a type popular between 1810 and 1820; the ornately framed looking glass of the 1860s is probably American. Next to the bed is a simple mahogany fall-front desk, made in either New York or Philadelphia about 1850.

Parlor of the Putnam-Balch House. The rococo revival leather-topped library table dates from about 1880. On the table is a four-branch, silver-plated brass candelabrum made in London about 1810, as well as a Bohemian amber glass decanter and two nineteenth-century Waterford glass decanters and glasses. The electrified gas chandelier came from a house in Falmouth, Maine, while the large gilded looking glass over the mantel was made in Boston about 1860. On the mantel are a pair of French brass candelabra of about 1860 and a gilt clock of about 1875 made in France for the Russian market. The elaborate Renaissance revival walnut cabinet to the left of the fireplace is attributed to Herter Brothers, dating to 1875–80.

overleaf
Drawing room of the Putnam-Balch House. Against
the back wall is an ebonized inlaid desk of about 1875
in the style of the Herter Brothers; the chair said to
have been used in the United States Senate. The set
of rosewood chairs was made in New York City
between 1865 and 1875. The tall walnut cabinet with
glass doors of about 1850 was once used in the library
of the Essex Institute and was probably made locally.
Next to the English repoussé brass wood box of about
1890 is an impressive Colonial revival mahogany tall-
case clock made by A. Stowell and Company of
Boston. In the center of the room is a Renaissance
revival marble-topped rosewood table of 1865–70 from
another Salem house.

Chesterwood, the summer retreat of sculptor Daniel
Chester French, built in the Berkshires, near
Stockbridge, Massachusetts, 1898, 1901. French
purchased the property in 1896 after his wife, Mary,
declared, "I do not know what you are going to do,
but I am going to live here." The studio, designed by
Henry Bacon of McKim, Mead & White, survives
intact, as does the family's Colonial revival house.
French met Bacon during the planning of the 1893
World's Columbian Exposition in Chicago. In the
course of their work on the fair and subsequent
commissions, French and Bacon became close
friends. They collaborated several decades later on
the Lincoln Memorial in Washington, Bacon as the
architect and French as the sculptor.

Fountain and semicircular marble-cement seat and
peony-bordered path outside the studio at
Chesterwood. French created a small formal garden
as an intimate forecourt to the entrance of his studio.

opposite
A sculpture by French on the grounds of
Chesterwood.

Naumkeag, the country house of Joseph Hodges Choate, Stockbridge, Massachusetts, designed by McKim, Mead & White and built in 1885–86. Naumkeag is the Indian word for "haven of rest" and was the Indian name for Salem, Massachusetts, Choate's birthplace. Stanford White superintended the building of the house and advised Mrs. Choate on the furnishings, while Nathaniel Barrett of Boston was the landscape architect. Choate served as the United States ambassador to England from 1899 to 1905, and passed the last years of his life at Naumkeag before his death in 1917. His daughter, Mabel, inherited the house and commissioned the Boston landscape architect Fletcher Steele to design gardens that reflected her interest in the Far East.

Steps lined with white birches at Naumkeag.
Fletcher Steele designed these steps to enable Mabel
Choate to reach the lower cutting garden more easily
in her declining years. As Miss Choate described the
stairs: "Instead of going straight down they divided
at the top into two tiers, turning back on themselves
with a gentle ramp, and between these tiers the
water came down from the black glass pool in a small
channel and into a basin with arched roof. There
were four of these tiers and basins. . . .The going
either up or down was no trouble at all."

Stair hall of Naumkeag. On the wall is a Flemish
tapestry of 1540–60 showing a hunt. The Hadley
chest from the Connecticut River Valley of 1690–1710
bears the initials "LE," probably for Lydia Eastman,
and said by family tradition to have been acquired
from Wallace Nutting in 1921. On the chest is a
Chinese bronze ceremonial bowl; the two rugs on the
floor are late-nineteenth-century Caucasian.

Joseph Choate's study at Naumkeag. Above the bookshelves on the right-hand wall hangs an 1895 engraving of Choate's cousin Rufus Choate, who recommended Joseph to his first law firm in 1855. Joseph Choate made his mark in the law, successfully arguing in 1895 that the graduated income tax was unconstitutional. In addition to the study, there is a library filled with Choate's books. Throughout the house are pieces of China Trade porcelain and other ceramics collected by the Choates' daughter, Mabel, who also acquired quantities of Oriental rugs that remain.

overleaf
Entrance hall of Naumkeag, Stockbridge. The portrait of Joseph Choate at the age of seventy-nine was painted by Ellen Emmet Rand. Under it is a Scottish oak settee inscribed "East or West Home is best" and the date "1636," although the settee is probably nineteenth century.

Bedroom at Naumkeag. The mixture of old and new at Naumkeag is characteristic of collectors after the Centennial of American Independence. Following the publication of Clarence Cook's *The House Beautiful* in 1878 and Charles Locke Eastlake's *Hints on Household Taste*, which went through eight American editions beginning in 1872, thoughtful Americans believed that beauty and taste were crucial in shaping character and shared the view that the general public was being degraded by tasteless, graceless mass-made products in their homes. These new collectors were seeking American antiques that would express the spirit and shed light on the daily habits of their forefathers. Antiques could not only represent the spirit of those earlier times but also transmit it with their fine workmanship, high-quality materials, and design.

The gardens at Naumkeag. The Chinese temple
pagoda (above) was designed by Fletcher Steele, who
worked on the gardens for some thirty years during
Mabel Choate's tenure. The pagoda was fashioned
from southern cast-iron work and then painted. It
shelters a rock on a Ming stone pedestal that had
been in the summer palace at Peking for three
centuries before Miss Choate brought them home
during her extensive travels in China.

above and opposite
The gardens at Naumkeag.

The William Cullen Bryant Homestead, Cummington, Massachusetts, built in 1785 and enlarged by Bryant around 1865. Bryant, the first American poet of international stature and for half a century the influential editor of one of America's oldest newspapers, the *New-York Evening Post*, was born here. The original house consisted of the top two floors of the present large central section. Bryant raised the original building and built a new ground floor below; the Palladian window on the second floor was once the front door. In 1872, Bryant's great-grandson Conrad Goddard described the property: "The site of the house is uncommonly beautiful. Before it, to the east, the ground descends first gradually and then rapidly, to the Westfield River flowing in a deep and narrow valley. . . Beyond it . . . the country rises again gradually, carrying the eye over a region of vast extent."

Study of the William Cullen Bryant Homestead. Bryant never found New York, with its cultivated amateurishness and dilettantism, a wholly congenial environment; the city had something of the atmosphere of Addisonian London and seemed far removed in spirit from the rural simplicity of his beloved Berkshire Hills. He returned in his mature years to the home of his youth, and in his later years he spent his mornings in this study translating Homer's *Iliad* and *Odyssey*, composing editorials for the *Post*, and writing some of his final verses.

overleaf
Entrance hall of Kingscote. The heavy Gothic moldings of the door are repeated in the arches separating the vestibule from the hall. The wall covering and paneled ceiling were installed when the house was renovated between 1876 and 1878.

Kingscote, Newport, Rhode Island, designed by Richard Upjohn for George Noble Jones of Savannah, Georgia, and built between 1839 and 1841. The service wing on the left was enlarged by George Champlin Mason and Son in 1877–78; three years later Stanford White designed the large addition between it and the original house. Although Newport had been a summering place since the early eighteenth century, there were few summer cottages in the 1830s. Genteel Southern families had long frequented Newport to escape the heat and malaria of their native region, and some had built houses in town. Jones was the first to select a piece of property well in the countryside for his summer place. His cottage and its location eventually inspired the craze that by end of the nineteenth century made Newport the most fashionable resort in the country. In 1863, Jones sold the house to William Henry King of Newport and it became known as Kingscote.

opposite
The dining room of Kingscote. Designed by Stanford White in 1881, the dining room incorporates many rich textures and patterns: cherry parquet flooring, mahogany wainscoting, cork-tiled ceiling, Siena marble facing on the fireplace surround, Tiffany glass tiles, and stained glass in the transoms. Borrowing from many styles he was then studying, White coherently combined Japanese, Moorish, English, Italian and Colonial American motifs with elements from the aesthetic movement. The result is one of his finest Queen Anne interiors in which rich light and dark textures are played against one another.

overleaf

North parlor of Kingscote. The silk damask wall covering, Louis XVI-style gilded furniture, and the elaborately carved Italian marble mantle were installed in 1880. The Oriental porcelain, hawthorn-root carvings, silk embroideries, and teak and lacquer objects throughout the house were acquired during the King family's years in the China Trade.

Château-sur-Mer, Newport, Rhode Island, built for William Shepherd Wetmore by the architect Seth Bradford in 1851–52 and completely remodeled by Richard Morris Hunt in 1871–78. This room was the main entrance hall until Hunt moved the front door to the north side of the house. The mahogany wainscoting and trim survive from the original 1852 building. The elaborate gold-leaf ceiling with stenciled and painted decoration in the Japanese taste dates from 1877 and gave this artful interior the high seriousness of the aesthetic movement. The Victorian tufted sofas are original to the hall.

opposite

Grand staircase of Château-sur-Mer. Hunt totally altered the plan of the house, which now centered around a soaring three-story hall. Another major feature of the new plan was this magnificent white-oak staircase, which rises four flights into the tower that he added to the north side of the house.

Library of Château-sur-Mer. The carved woodwork of the walls, ceiling, library table and bookcases were made by a Florentine craftsman and installed in this room by Hunt. The portrait above the fireplace is of George Peabody, the international banker, financier, and philanthropist who was William Shepard Wetmore's business partner.

Dining room of Château-sur-Mer. The walls are covered with the same tooled, gilded, and painted leather that upholsters the chairs. The centerpiece on the table is part of a monumental silver *surtout-de-table* depicting the Judgment of Paris, made by Paul Storr of London in 1822.

overleaf
Edith Keteltas Wetmore's bedroom at Château-sur-Mer. Soon after William Shepard Wetmore completed the original portion of the house in 1851–52, his wife, a young beauty, left her young family for the thrills of Europe on the arm of one of her husband's coachmen. Wetmore died in 1862, leaving the house and the bulk of his estate to his sixteen-year-old son, George Peabody Wetmore. In 1869 George Peabody Wetmore married Edith Keteltas, a member of a prominent New York and Newport family, and the following year retained Richard Morris Hunt to enlarge his house. The portrait on the easel beside the fireplace is of George Peabody Wetmore, painted by his cousin Julian Story in 1892.

George Peabody Wetmore's bedroom at Château-sur-Mer. The Wetmores spent most of the decade of the 1870s in England while Hunt worked on the house. There they spent much of their time shopping for furnishings in the latest fashion. The arts and crafts style, which was flourishing in the hands of William Morris, was England's most avant-garde at the time, and the Wetmores purchased this wallpaper he designed. The bed is part of a four-piece suite of red-stained and ebonized furniture made by Gregory and Company in 1876.

Butternut room at Château-sur-Mer. The seventeen-piece suite of butternut furniture was one of two sets ordered by George Peabody Wetmore from Léon Marcotte in 1869 and bears Wetmore's monogram. The wallpaper was reproduced from remnants of the original French wallpaper found on the walls of the room; the griffin frieze was designed by the English arts and crafts artist William Burges. Above the mantel hangs *Homage Paid to Charles V by the Knights of the Golden Fleece*, painted by Albrecht Frans Lievin De Vriendt about 1875.

Lockwood-Mathews Mansion, Norwalk, Connecticut, built by LeGrand Lockwood in 1869, designed and decorated by the Paris-trained Detlef Lienau and Léon Marcotte, and owned after 1876 by Charles D. Mathews. The sixty-room mansion is a rich expression of nineteenth-century eclecticism, combining elements of a French Renaissance château and a Scottish manor house with a taste for Victorian plush. Lockwood, who had made his fortune in railroad investments, shipping, and trading in stocks and bonds, was the first millionaire of Norwalk and built one of the costliest and most elaborate mansions in America at the time. Lockwood himself scoured the Old World in search of marbles, rare woods, metal, stone, and objects of art to embellish the house. He imported Egyptian porphyry and Florentine marble carved to his order in Italy. The finest of exotic and native woods, all carved, inlaid, and gilded, were used for the interior trim and furnishings. Murals, wood sculptures, marble statues, and contemporary paintings added to the princely setting. In 1873 the *New York Sun* reported that it was perhaps "the most perfect and elegant mansion in America."

The Mark Twain House, in Hartford, Connecticut. In 1873, Samuel Langhorne Clemens, better known under the pen name Mark Twain, purchased land at the western edge of the city in an area known as Nook Farm. He engaged the New York architect Edward Tuckerman Potter to design his house, which was completed in 1874. The architect exploited the decorative possibilities of various courses, and then further embellished the surface with a bold pattern of black and vermilion paint. The elaborate treatment of the wood structural members and railing is characteristic of the Stick Style of the 1870s. He extended the bay windows up to form turrets, the top floor of which became open porches for a relaxed enjoyment of the view.

opposite
Entrance hall of the Mark Twain House. Originally neo-Tudor in style, with ornamental details carved by Léon Marcotte of New York and Paris, the front hall was given a completely different character by the Associated Artists (Samuel Colman, Lockwood de Forest, and Candace Wheeler) in 1881. The paneling was stenciled in silver to give the effect of mother-of-pearl inlay, the walls and ceiling painted red and patterned in dark blue. These patterns, which resemble North American Indian textiles, probably were designed by Louis C. Tiffany. To William Dean Howells, the house represented Twain's "love of magnificence as if it had been another sealskin coat, and he was at the crest of the prosperity which enabled him to humor every whim or extravagance."

198

overleaf

Library of the Mark Twain House, painted peacock blue by the Associated Artists in 1881. Twain bought the the great ceiling-high Scottish mantel in 1874 from Ayton Castle near Edinburgh, made for the Mitchell-Innes family, whose crests appear in the overmantel. Twain had the dedicatory inscription and the date 1869 removed and added the date of his own house, 1874. Here he read to his family from his own manuscripts, and from Shakespeare and the Brownings and told his daughters stories about each of the objects carved on the mantel. Of this room Twain wrote in 1892: "How ugly, tasteless, repulsive are all the domestic interiors I have ever seen in Europe compared with the perfect taste of this ground floor, with its delicious dream of harmonious color, and its all-pervading spirit of peace and serenity and deep contentments."

Nineteenth-century American furniture in the John Tarrant Kenney Hitchcock Museum, Riverton, Connecticut. The museum building is the former Episcopal Union Church built in 1829 on property once owned by Lambert Hitchcock. At his famous factory, Hitchcock mass-produced painted and grained "fancy" furniture made of local woods and decorated with freehand and stenciled designs. At the peak of his success, Hitchcock employed more than a hundred workers, including women and children who painted and stenciled on the assembly line. Hitchcock chairs—a type then known to the trade as "fancy chairs"—were turned out in prodigious numbers, sold for $1.50 retail, and were a stock in trade of many a wandering Yankee peddler.

View from the sitting room into the formal gardens at Hildene, the home of Robert Todd Lincoln, Manchester Village, Vermont. The gardens have been restored to their original beauty. Many of the original plantings remain, and the site on a promontory in the valley provides a striking panoramic view of the Green and Taconic mountain ranges and the Battenkill Valley below. For six months of every year, Robert Lincoln ran the Pullman Company from Hildene until he retired in 1911. The files of his personal papers and books remain for the most part exactly where they were when he died in 1926.

opposite
Dining room of Hildene, designed by the Boston architectural firm of Shepley, Rutan and Coolidge and built between 1903 and 1905. Robert, the only son of Abraham and Mary Todd Lincoln to survive to maturity, became a successful attorney in Chicago, was appointed secretary of war by President James Garfield, served as minister to Great Britain under President Benjamin Harrison, and eventually was chosen president and chairman of the board of the Pullman Company. In 1902, at the height of his corporate career, Robert Lincoln sought refuge in the mountains of Vermont and built Hildene, "hill and valley."

The kitchen at Hildene. Almost as many rooms were provided for servants and service as for the family. The kitchen is dominated by the old cast-iron stove in which either coal or wood may be burned.

Wilson Castle, Proctor, Vermont, built in the middle of the nineteenth century in the heart of the Green Mountains and home of five generations of the Wilson family. The English brick and Vermont marble facade is dominated by nineteen open proscenium arches and shadowed by a towering turret, parapet, and balcony. Inside are thirty-two rooms filled with an eclectic assortment of art treasures and furniture from abroad. European art was an index of cultural refinement, some maintained; hence it was a simple matter for Americans of taste and refinement to come abreast of the older nations. "What is fine in the buildings of the old countries," observed the editor of *Harper's Magazine* in 1859, "we can borrow; their statues and their pictures we will be able in good time to buy." It was a prophetic statement. Not many years later, architects enriched by years of study abroad returned to build Renaissance "palaces" for wealthy American clients.

Grand stairwell alcove of Wilson Castle, paneled in mahogany and with three large stained–glass cathedral windows. On the landing is a small reed organ.

Dining room of Wilson Castle, Proctor, Vermont. Built in the Renaissance revival style of oak paneling, the room is filled with art objects from a great variety of nations and periods. The layering and juxtaposition of many different patterns and the use of a subtle palette of colors demonstrated a heightened artistic consciousness on the part of the decorators and at the same time demanded of the owner a refined sensibility. Each object or detail deserved close attention, yet, like a mosaic, the whole became unified when seen from a distance.

Farm barn of Shelburne Farms in Vermont's
Champlain Valley, Shelburne Farms was created by
Dr. William Seward Webb and his wife, Elza (Lila)
Osgood Vanderbilt Webb, who began construction of
the landscape elements and buildings in 1886 and
continued over the next fifteen years. William Seward
Webb envisioned a modernization of agriculture not
unlike the modernization that so profoundly changed
industry during his lifetime. He insisted that modern
technology be used wherever possible. Thus, the farm
barn's steam-powered elevators carried grain and
straw from floor to floor, gaslights were installed in
nearly every building, and telegraph lines linked the
farm barn and Shelburne House to the rest of the
world. Standing four stories tall, the farm building is
407 feet long by 117 feet wide, which at the time of its
construction was the largest barn in the country.
Gifford Pinchot, the father of American forestry,
visited the farms several times and served as a
consultant in the forestry activities.

opposite
Coach barn of Shelburne Farms, designed by New
York architect Robert Henderson Robertson and
built in 1901–02. Shelburne Farms originally
encompassed about four thousand acres—over six
square miles. Frederick Law Olmsted provided the
outline of the estate's design by organizing the
property into three spaces: farm, forest, and
parkland. Webb constructed the estate as an
experiment in which new techniques in land use,
horse breeding, and dairying were employed.
Believing that a good road horse was preferable to an
indifferent trotter, he laid before the farmers of
Vermont for many years the superior advantages of
English hackneys and French coach horses for
country use and for market over the farmers' loyalty
to the old Morgan stock.

The Goodspeed Opera House, East Haddam, Connecticut, built in 1876–77 by William Goodspeed, an entrepreneur whose interests included shipping and shipbuilding and a true love of theater. One of the handsomest of a handful of Victorian theaters that have survived in this country, the Goodspeed is today a fully equipped performing theater. The Connecticut River, which flows past the Opera House, was the highway of the early colonists, and the valley began to attract English settlers as early as 1635. The Goodspeed Landing buildings flourished until the turn of the century, when the advent of the railroad caused a decline in activity along the river and in the prosperity of the Opera House and village.

The Grand Isle, a private railroad car built in 1890, at Shelburne Museum, Shelburne, Vermont. William Seward Webb was president of the Wagner Palace Coach Company, owned by his father-in-law, William Henry Vanderbilt, who also owned the New York Central. Webb visited Vermont in 1881 on business, scouting Vermont rail lines and prospects for his father-in-law, and consequently discovered the beauties of the state, and of Shelburne Point in particular. Webb subsequently build the Adirondack division of the New York Central and ran the Rutland Railroad, a prosperous feeder for the New York Central. The elegantly decorated Grand Isle was built by the Wagner Palace Coach Company and presented by Webb in 1890 to the Governor of Vermont, Edward C. Smith.

The Age of Expansion in the Frontier West

Frontiers Transformed

THE WEST WAS ONCE ALL AMERICA. By the end of the Revolution, its eastern boundary had retreated to the Appalachians; by 1815, it meant Kentucky, Tennessee, the "Old Northwest," and areas along the lower Mississippi. Beyond that river lay the vague unknown of the Louisiana Purchase. By 1861, citizens of Wisconsin or Ohio were "western men" but the West, slowly metamorphosing into the Great West, meant the trans-Mississippi world. On the eve of the Civil War, much of the United States beyond the Mississippi River was still unexplored or only dimly known. On the eastern fringe, where civilization ended and wilderness began, was a tier of rough border states— Minnesota in the north, then Iowa, Missouri, Arkansas, Louisiana, Texas, and, finally, Kansas, which was admitted to the Union only a few weeks before Lincoln's inauguration. Large areas of these states were still unsettled, lacking roads and other marks of the white man. Stretching for almost two thousand miles was a spacious land of awesome distances and immense skies, of buffalo-covered plains, great rivers, red-rock canyons, waterless badlands and deserts, and dark, forested mountain ranges whose granite peaks gleamed year-round with snow. Extremes characterized the country. The Great West was an area at once beautiful and brutal, alluring and destructive, fertile and desolate, full of unparalleled wonders and incredible hardships for which nothing had prepared immigrants.

Size was greater, distance longer, mountains higher, canyons deeper, unshaded plains more terrifying or beautiful, deserts more hazardous than anyone had dreamed. Nature was a perpetual surprise, a continuous revelation, an endless peril, and a furtive trap.

Ever since Lewis and Clark had first crossed and written about the West in the early years of the century, explorers and popular writers had portrayed the country beyond the Mississippi and Missouri rivers largely in wondrous terms of romance and drama. So long as Romanticism shaped attitudes in the late eighteenth and early nineteenth centuries, the untamed wilderness of the West would be seen as a purifying Eden where men were cleansed of their sins by nearness to their Creator. The North American Indian could be viewed as the most envied of all people, bathed in righteousness and free of oppression—a true Noble Savage to be envied and imitated. Even the most ardent Rousseauist realized that this idealized image could not long endure, but few could anticipate the violence of the revolution in thought that toppled the Noble Savage from his pedestal as the age of romance gave way to the age of utilitarianism in the early years of the nineteenth century. The Indian's demise was hastened by the reports of hostile travelers and disillusioned visitors from Europe, nurtured on the Noble Savage tradition, expecting to find godlike Children of Nature living amid abundance and freedom. What they found instead were primitive people just emerging from the Stone Age whom they described as dirty, slovenly, lazy uncultured barbarians.

An emerging generation of government-sponsored explorers deepened the shadow. In 1823, Major Stephen H. Long pronounced the central plains a Great American Desert, whose sparse rainfall, scarcity of wood and water, and apparent infertility—inferred from the vast treeless expanses—would make them "uninhabitable by a people depending on agriculture for their subsistence." Others wrote and spoke luridly of the "howling" western wilderness, of strange and perilous landscapes, blizzards, high winds and violent electrical storms, ferocious grizzly bears, and, always, hostile red men. The new mood vastly altered the image of the frontier; the forests and the grasslands of the West were transformed from beckoning Edens to forbidding barriers to progress—hostile, evil, unwanted—existing only to be destroyed. The result was a multifaceted image of successive American Wests: hostile or friendly, peaceful or warlike, beautiful or ugly, inviting or repelling, as the whims and prejudices of the image-makers dictated.

From their beginnings, Americans in the East have been westering peoples. From the lecture platform of the Concord Lyceum in 1851, Henry David Thoreau captured in a few ringing words the whole story of westward expansion and the frontier process: "Eastward I go only by force; but westward I go free . . . in Wildness is the preservation of the World." By the 1840s, the frontier of settlement was emerging on the lush grasslands of the western Mississippi Valley and the interminable Great Plains of the Far West. Inexorably, the strong lures of opportunity and reward, and a belief in the country's destiny to expand to the Pacific Ocean, uprooted men and families from comfort and safety in the East to risk their lives and property in the West. To the pious and romantic, the awesome emptiness and limitless horizons of the prairies and plains were the ultimate symbols of God's presence, humbling mere humans by their infinite magnitude. To others, the huge western reaches were barren wastelands, overwhelming in their vastness, their emptiness defying the puny efforts of man. On the trails were emigrant families and fortune hunters, pack strings of traders and merchants, trains of ox-drawn freight wagons, drovers with herds of bawling livestock, Army units, and an occasional speeding stagecoach filled with passengers and mail. The major trunk routes—the Santa Fe and California and Oregon trails—were already rich in history and folklore. The Mormons were turning the desert green on the edge of Utah's Great Salt Lake, and fleets of covered wagons were carrying the household possessions of families of young and old to new homes in Oregon. A rash of gold and silver rushes had swelled the westward movement, and in the 1850s many previously unmapped pockets in the mountains and deserts had become known. Still, by the time of Lincoln's inauguration, fewer than five million of his fellow Americans—about 14 percent of the country's population—lived west of the Mississippi River, and 80 percent of them were concentrated in Missouri and the other border states east of the Great Plains. Easterners, particularly New Englanders, were migrating during the 1850s, but they moved to regions where life and property were secure, planting churches and schools along the way.

Journeying along the National Road through Pennsylvania in 1817, Morris Birkbeck noted that with many families, "a small wagon (so light that you might almost carry it, yet strong enough to bear a good load of bedding, utensils and provisions, and a swarm of young citizens and to sustain marvelous shocks in its passage over these rocky heights), with two small horses, sometimes a cow or two, comprises their all; excepting a little store of hard-earned cash for the land office of the district, where they may obtain a title for as many acres as they possess half-dollars, being one fourth of the purchase money. The wagon has tilt, or cover, made of a sheet, or perhaps a blanket. The family are seen before, behind, or within the vehicle, according to the road or the weather, or perhaps the spirits of the party."

Frontier Americans were vulgar, according to reports of visiting Europeans. They were materialistic, avaricious, selfish, boastful, rude, gluttonous, cruel, violent. Other travelers disagreed: Americans were friendly, generous, helpful, natural, unspoiled, hospitable, affectionate. Western frontier people were long depicted as rugged individualists, but these same individualists were also resolute collectivists in joining with their spouses and children in clearing land and building homesteads, with their townspeople in cabin raisings, logrollings, law enforcing, with authorities in laying roads, fighting Indians, erecting forts, financing schools. Western settlers, who were supposed to be materialistic, set up schools and churches, libraries and literary societies, almost as fast as they established saloons and stables. On the whole, they were more daring, more restless, more mobile, more middle-income than the rest of the population. They were also generally outsiders who sought the West to escape a society in which distinctions of birth and possession had put them at a disadvantage. Class lines existed along the frontier, but they were less firmly drawn and more easily breached than in older communities in the East.

The hallmark of frontier people was diversity. They were diverse in their environments, settling in behind a constantly moving frontier while hunters and trappers were advancing ahead of it. They were diverse in occupation: speculators, merchants, lawyers, farmers, riverboat men, blacksmiths, flour millers, road builders, printers, distillers, teachers. They were self-contradictory, now friendly and now suspicious, generous and stingy, religious and blasphemous, nationalistic and parochial, hardworking and self-indulgent, rowdy and respectable. They were ambitious but lacking in lofty ambition, observers concluded. The frontier acted as a safety valve for the East and helped reshape American character, making western society more fluid than European. Western outposts stimulated the spirit of individualism and inventiveness, putting a special premium on democracy and versatility, and fostered the particularly American traits of earthiness and practicality. Along the frontier, an atmosphere of progress and the "go-ahead" spirit prevailed, influencing men and their institutions.

Beyond the Frontier

West of the great bend of the Missouri lay an immense wilderness described by the school geographies as the "Great American Desert" because of its inhospitable terrain and climate. Once the white population took over the country east of the Mississippi, the displaced North American Indians were forced to move to these central plains and a land known for the most extreme temperature range in the United States. This was country the whites would "never" want, in which the Indians might pitch their tents and hunt the buffalo for time everlasting. Wilderness and Indians were seen as fit companions and bringing them together in the West seemed a fine and philanthropic solution to Easterners. The new policy developed slowly, but it was stated clearly as early as 1825. All eastern tribes were to be given land west of the Mississippi as "permanent home, and which shall, under the most solemn guarantee of the United States, be, and remain theirs forever." A commissioner of Indian affairs—a member of the War Department—was given supervision of the Indians. Eastern Indians greeted these neat plans and firm promises with anything but enthusiasm, expressing unexpected devotion to the lands of their fathers, their cornfields, and hunting grounds. But resistance, they saw, meant only extermination.

Americans in general approved the governmental policy, holding it was the kindest possible method of acquiring the land that God had designated for white use. It was "Manifest Destiny," expansion, prearranged by heaven, over an area not clearly defined. In some minds it meant expansion over the region to the Pacific Ocean; in others, over the North American continent; in still others, over the whole hemisphere. The idea of the frontier as a boundary had hardly been imbedded in the popular mind before it ceased to exist, as the Great Plains proved no barrier to white ambition. The promises of the United States government to Indians proved worthless in the end. Occupation was the moral force that should, and would, move territory into the American orbit. A free, confederated, self-governed republic on a continental scale—this was Manifest Destiny. One other text was part of the gospel of Manifest Destiny: the duty of the United States to regenerate backward peoples of the continent. "The Indians in due course must either become civilized or be shot," one Army officer in the West declared. The Indian was a heathen whose land title passed, according to canon well established, to the Christian prince and his heirs who had discovered and conquered him. Natives retained only rights of occupancy on their diminished lands, limited to government-designated reservations.

Before 1865, the trans-Mississippi West went through a significant transition from frontier, or sequential frontiers, to region, a shift from relative newness to relative oldness, from flux to fixity. At its heart, the transition was a process of creating new, stabler geographic identities in the midst of vast landscapes that people chose to perceive as home. Perhaps the most telling sign of this transition was a feeling among the inhabitants of a place they were no longer inventing but inheriting. Lands seized from Indians to be held under one legal system, territorial boundaries defined on a national map, state forming, and the sense of citizen selfhood that flows from American nationalism—all suggest the success of the Old World invasion of the New. The Great West then and now has regional identity that sets it apart from the rest of the continent: its general aridity, low population density, intense contrast between urban and rural landscapes. More than anywhere else in North America, the regional self-identity of the West flows from its ties to the past. It was the last frontier.

In three decades—from 1865 until 1890, when the Bureau of the Census announced that the frontier was closed—successive waves of pioneers settled more territory than their eastern predecessors had done in 250 years. Between 1607 and 1870, 409 million acres of land had been settled and 189 million acres were cultivated, but between 1870 and 1900, 430 million acres were settled and 225 million acres were cultivated.

The fabled western fur trappers lived an exhilarating life, lonely, wild, and perilous. Scorching sun, blizzards, hostile Indians, and grizzly bears were routine hazards. The principal attraction of this vast domain was its wealth of furs, which commanded high prices in the world markets. The frenzied search for beaver swept these men into every cranny, making them unintentional explorers of vast territory. The trappers discovered most of the geographic secrets of the region. The mountain trade was significant in another respect: it disguised territorial rivalries of nations whose companies competed for the trade. Territorial domination was the ultimate goal of this trade, just as it had been of the eastern fur-trade rivalries during the colonial period. The region fought over in this rivalry was immense—the equivalent of half of Europe was in contest. California and the southern intermountain plateau areas in the Southwest, possessions of Spain but held by a feeble and ineffective grasp, were seized by the United States between 1846 and 1848 in the Mexican War. The Oregon Country up to the 49th parallel was acquired at about the same time. The total territory thus obtained was 800,000 square miles. In all modern history, there have been no rivalries or seizures comparable to these except those of the European powers in Africa and China.

The mountain fur trade also led to agricultural settlement of the Far West by Americans. The trappers who survived the dangers of their calling seldom ever returned to their eastern homes; wild freedom had made them unfit for civilized living. When they were too old to be effective trappers, the mountain men settled in some far western locality, especially on the rich bottom lands in the Willamette Valley of the Oregon Country or the Central Valley of California. These choice regions were turned to farming by the former trappers, who thus initiated the process of American pioneer occupation. Finally, the fur trade was significant in the growth of St. Louis, which became the greatest primary fur market in the United States and one of the largest in the world. Alone, the mountain man had explored this vast land, mastered its tangled geography, mapped its routes, opened trade with the Indian tribes—most of whom had never seen a white man before—and prepared the way for the first wave of pioneers. But by the time covered-wagon emigrants rolled into the Great American Desert and made that great territory home, the mountain man was a forgotten footnote in the history of the West.

The Great Surge

In the years preceding the Civil War, the far western territories became the scene of a new frontier advance, that of miners, which turned the United States into one of the world's greatest producers of precious metals. In the 1820s, American interest in California, then a province of Mexico, was in the hide and tallow trade. Boston ships traded cutlery, finery, and Yankee notions for tallow, which was shipped to Peru to be turned into candles for use in homes and in silver mines. Hides went to New England harness and shoe manufacturers. (The classic account of this trade is Richard Henry Dana's *Two Years Before the Mast*.) In 1846, there were only five to eight hundred Americans in California.

Then came the California Gold Rush, the biggest and richest of the gold strikes. It all began, as every schoolchild is taught, one January day in 1848 at the sawmill of John Sutter in the valley of the Sacramento. As word of the discovery spread, San Francisco became almost hysterical. Even among experienced westerners, the frenzy and madness was acute. "The whole country," wrote one San Francisco newspaper editor, "resounds with the sordid cry of Gold! Gold! Gold! while the field is left half planted, the house half built, and everything neglected but the manufacture of shovels and pick-axes." As the fever spread to other California settlements, ranches were deserted, grain went unharvested, cattle and horses roamed wild. Sailors deserted their ships and soldiers their posts. The Spanish alcalde of Monterey described the situation there: "All were off for the mines, some on horses, some on carts, and some on crutches, and one went in a litter." Ships carried the news to the Sandwich Islands (Hawaii), and during the summer nineteen vessels left in three weeks for the Pacific shores. The Argonauts from the Atlantic states, as the gold seekers inevitably came to be called, had a choice of two sea routes to San Francisco: the all-water route around Cape Horn or the shorter and faster, but more miserable, crossing of the Isthmus of Panama. One conservative estimate suggests that during 1849, seven hundred seventy-five vessels sailed from Eastern ports for California. Eighty thousand miners poured into the territory, and by the end of 1852, a special census set the state's population at 223,856.

New surges to the diggings soon followed. To those living in the Mississippi Valley, the natural route was overland, and there were even gold seekers from the eastern seaboard states who joined these wagon companies. Land travelers had a choice of routes including various southern routes, such as the Sonora Trail that swings down into Mexico, and the Santa Fe Trail, then either looped into southern California by the Old Spanish Trail through Utah or dropped southwest to the Gila River. But the overwhelming majority followed the Oregon and Mormon trails, which parallel each other on opposite sides of the Platte River over the Great Plains; once through the Rockies, they swung down toward the California passes along various routes and cutoffs—none of them easy. In 1849 and 1850, the villain along this stretch of the trail was not hardship but a cholera epidemic that was ravaging the Mississippi Valley. The trip had a rigid timetable. Travelers began gathering in March at three Missouri River towns that became the outfitting places for the overland trip: Independence and St. Joseph, Missouri, and Council Bluffs (then called Kanesville by the Mormons who founded the town), Iowa. The different strands knit together in the Platte Valley near Fort Kearney, built in 1848. The wagons could not start before late April, when the grass on the prairie was green and high enough to provide food for the teams, and they had to be over the Sierra Nevada in California before snow began to fall in the high passes. Tens of thousands came by the overland trails until 1859. That was the year the great Comstock Lode was discovered in what is now Nevada. Virtually every miner in California dropped what he was doing and headed through the passes of the Sierra Nevada to the new Eldorado. Almost overnight, a roaring, miserable collection of tents and shanties called Virginia City sprang up on the inhospitable sides of the barren peak. The great Comstock Lode, was worked at first for gold but proved later to contain an immense body of silver, which was the source of many great American fortunes—those of the Hearsts, the Millses, the Mackays, the Floods, and others.

New Empires and New Men

Once the whole of the West was under United States control, emigration surged. As more of the best land in Oregon and California was settled, the westering urge at last found its object closer to home, on the much maligned grasslands of the Plains. Important to this shift was the

Kansas-Nebraska Act of 1854, which turned the two future states into federal territories and opened them officially to settlers. And the settlers came, particularly out of the valleys of the lower Ohio and lower Missouri. The motive of the land rush was largely economic; the emigrants settled in the prize portion of Kansas—the more fertile eastern section—in response to the normal pioneer desire to take advantage of prairie soils. As tens of thousands of pioneers—fifty to sixty thousand annually in the 1850s—moved across the plains and mountains to Oregon and California on the wagon trails, the need for a transcontinental railroad was soon evident. This would tie California to the rest of the union, integrating that distant coast more closely and safely to the heartland of the nation, as well as reaching across the plains and mountains to ensure commercial ties to the Orient. An obliging United States government provided congressional legislation to enable visionary railroad builders to obtain loans. Federal homesteading boons combined with railroad-industry blandishments drew to the West ever more farmers and would-be farmers whose interests often conflicted with those of cattle barons and dirt-poor cowboys who worked for them. Women came, too, to raise children, labor alongside their husbands in the fields, or eke out a hardscrabble living in distant mining camps. Into the mix poured many honest small businessmen hoping to get in on the ground floor of boomtowns, a fair helping of drifters and adventurers, and a goodly number of scoundrels. It was a Wild West indeed—this flat, wind-swept, treeless expanse of the Great Plains, a region that stretched from Canada to the Texas Panhandle, from the Missouri River to the Rocky Mountains.

The era also experienced a swift advance of farming across the prairie province and into the Great Plains. By 1870, the limit of frontier civilization lay at the edge of the Great Plains, where an American character was formed—a people audacious and self-reliant and naive, generous and stubborn, righteous but forgiving, humorous in a folksy way, violent, hospitable, contradictory. It advanced despite the strains and fatalities of the war in the South. This rapid spread of population and scattered settlements meant that the Middle West between 1860 and 1880 became an enormous grain-growing community that supported the corn kingdom—an empire of hogs and pork production that made Cincinnati and Chicago rivals for primacy as meat-packing centers.

The hunger for land was even more acute in the restless times following the Civil War. Returning Union army veterans now found their home in the North too cramped and life there unpromising. Former Rebels felt an even greater need of a fresh start; many had come back from the war to find their homes destroyed, their livestock gone, their fields and orchards returned to the wild, their way of life lost, and their country in the hands of Yankee occupation forces and carpetbaggers. From the Old South, too, came a new kind of American citizen—the freed slave—who burned to be a landowner and farmer. And from across the Atlantic came thousands of northern European immigrants, driven out of their native countries by poverty, political oppression, and religious persecution and lured to the American prairie by the promise of land that was trumpeted as a bounteous Eden.

This enormous expansion was the product of a combination of forces, including the Homestead Act of 1862, which offered grants of 160 acres to anyone twenty-one years of age or older. The homesteader had only to build a shelter within the first six months and make improvements during the next five years, after which he or she could "prove up" fulfillment of the legal requirements and gain full title to the property. Another force behind the great migration was the realization that the era of well-watered free land was drawing to a close; in 1880, the Director of the Census warned that the era of free land was ending. A third factor was the attractive prices of school lands, university lands, and other state lands that were put on the market in competition with homesteads. And this flow of settlement was stimulated by easy-credit conditions; investment capital in western farm mortgages was plentiful in the East.

The railroads were the chief factor in this swift colonization. The Transcontinental Railroad Act of 1862 had granted them vast stretches of government land in wide strips along the track, giving them large tracts to sell. Colonization was advertised with extraordinary enthusiasm, with hundreds of agents distributing literature in various European countries and receiving immigrants in

New York City. They offered special immigrant rates to the West and advised new arrivals on settlement and the best methods of farming. The Northern Pacific brought in Scandinavian immigrants, while the Atchison, Topeka, and Santa Fe attracted German Mennonites from Russia. These railroads were not always scrupulous in their methods; they permitted their New York agents to use dubious means of luring immigrants and were said to have stolen trainloads of immigrants from each other. High-pressure salesmanship was used to dispose of lands. Claiming a homestead was often not the realization of a settler's dreams but the beginning of his worst troubles. Rapturous tales were told of what the land would grow, but easterners, familiar only with fertile soil and abundant rainfall, never considered that a grant of 160 acres might not even provide a family's subsistence in the arid West. The climate of the plains was misrepresented by gaudy railroad come-ons that did not mention summer temperatures might exceed 110 degrees with no shade for miles around, or that winter temperatures dropped more than 40 degrees below zero, with blinding blizzards that could catch a man out in the open and leave him lost and frozen a few feet from his door. Nature offered a seemingly endless procession of other tests of the body, spirit, and even sanity. Furious and violent tornadoes, unceasing wind, lightning, hailstorms, prairie fires, flash floods, and grasshopper plagues threatened crops, livestock, and human life itself. But of all the capricious difficulties the settlers had to face, the two most lethal were debt and drought on the Plains. Many emigrants had borrowed money for the train fare west or for their most basic farming needs—a yoke of oxen, or a pair of mules, a wagon, a plow, and seed—and anything that went awry could wipe them out. Ultimately, the settlers were held hostage to the fate of climatic cycles.

For most newly arrived families, the first priority was to get a crop in the ground. The work was slow and hard. So solid was the earth that the cast-iron plow in use back East could make little headway in breaking the soil; a sharp-edged plow of steel or tempered iron with a different curvature was required. Once their plows broke the virgin sod for the first time, the settlers began to sow much the same crops they had planted east of the Missis-sippi. Corn, cotton, flax, oats, and other grains constituted the overwhelming contents of their storehouses at the end of harvest, with climate and soil determining what would be grown. And, of course, every farm had its own subsistence vegetable garden providing produce for the farmer's table.

The movement to the Plains was not a steady progress but one of fits and starts, with a brief rush here and another there. The settlers at first followed the fertile river valleys where the land was more level and the water more immediately available; then they settled along the railroads and gradually spread across the Plains to the Rockies, into and through its more tillable lowlands, spilling out on the other side.

By the 1870s, the life of the boom-or-bust sodbusters began to improve through technological advances. One of the first was an inexpensive factory-made windmill designed to pivot so it always faced the shifting wind. Taking advantage of the region's one inexhaustible energy source, these windmills ensured ample water for livestock and saved women the backbreaking toil of raising and carrying water for washing and cooking. Close in the wake of windmills came barbed wire, invented in 1873 by an Illinois farmer by the name of J. F. Glidden. On land lacking both wood and stone, barbed wire fences revolutionized life on the plains, foreshadowing the end of open-range cattle ranching and giving homesteaders a cheap and sure method of protecting their crops from destruction by hungry cows or the dwindling buffalo herds. Technology also came to farmwork. Breaking the sod first with a simple plow pulled by two animals, the successful farmer slowly graduated to ganged plows pulled by larger teams. Reaping, binding, and threshing machines followed, powered first by great numbers of draft animals, then by stationary steam engines. Finally, steam tractors completed the mechanization of agriculture.

Frontier Community

Almost in the shadow of the relentless push and containment of the Indian and largely removed from the opportunism of the gold and fur seekers, a teeming new white civilization sprouted almost as soon as trees fell to axes and sod felt the slice of the plow. As farm families became more numerous, the Great Plains began to fill up and towns grew to meet their need for access to market facilities, gristmills, railroads, manufactured goods from the East, medical care, schooling, and religion. Initially, it was peoples of English-speaking background who came West—Englishmen, Scots and a few Welsh—along with a few Swiss and French Huguenots, some Germans in Missouri and Texas, and a smattering of others. But as the West opened up, more and more immigrants from across the Atlantic arrived to stake their claim. The political upheavals in Europe in the 1840s and 1850s saw huge numbers of expatriates go West to seek a second chance. In some places, these new settlers presented a babel of tongues and myriad social and cultural peculiarities. Literally millions of Germans and Scandinavians arrived after the Civil War; almost all were poor, with nothing but their clothing, and almost all craved one thing—land. The Germans embarked from St. Louis and started to spread westward along the Missouri River, constructing tidy little clusters of homes and farm buildings with a German sense of orderliness. This, in turn, created a comfortable atmosphere for other new arrivals from the old country resulting in substantial communities that lent a distinctive flavor to some towns on the American frontier.

As far-flung communities grew in size, the increased sense of social kinship and shared values among their members gave rise to permanent institutions such as schools and churches. The first scattered homesteaders had to teach their children the basics at home, but as soon as a community of settlers could raise enough money, they put up a one-room schoolhouse and hired a teacher. But for all the importance homesteading families placed on education, their need for help on the farm made serious inroads into time to attend school. Students might come to classes for a few months in a row, then drop out for a year or more. Where there was a school there would soon be a church, followed by a Grange hall, a farm-machinery dealership, a theater or opera house, and other amenities. The Great Plains were just as majestic and as intimidating as ever, but they were no longer the undisturbed realm of nomadic Indians, buffalo, prairie dogs, and grass. By untold strug-

gle and immeasurable courage and grit, the men and women who came West set the course for America's heartland that would make the Great American Desert the most productive agricultural land on earth. The people tended to be of an optimistic and hopeful nature, but they were also often woefully naive about what lay in store. Even after a pioneer staked his claim and settled down, the struggle was far from over. To those accustomed to the wooded, hilly country back East, the flat expanse of the prairie was dismaying. And the recurring prairie fires and dust storms that leveled crops and destroyed houses bludgeoned more than one would-be farmer. But most settlers stuck it out, forging new lives and communities in the vast land they now called home.

To a remarkable extent, these first emigrants were people who had already moved; some had moved several times before crossing the Mississippi. There were large families moving again and again within a generation to improve their holdings; there were single young men who struck out to the West to make a place for themselves and perhaps to find a wife on the frontier; and there were whole colonies who moved together and settled en masse to form instant communities. These people were not rejecting society by coming to the wilderness; rather, they were turning their backs on a society that had failed them—economically, culturally, religiously, or socially— and came to build a new one in its place.

First they had to build their own piece of that society, and that meant a house. The variety of structures that went up on the plains and prairies was as great as the imaginations of the builders, divided by the building materials available. At its most rudimentary, the first home was the inside of the wagon that brought their possessions west with them. Tents sprouted on the grasslands in summer and fall but they, too, were temporary. Finding building materials was a challenge on the plains, where settlers found land that was, in the words of one new Kansan, "bare, treeless, wind swept, sun scorched." When timber was not available, the pioneers turned to the earth beneath their feet, hacking through the tough roots of prairie grass to chop out heavy sod bricks. With bare ground as the floor, these houses had walls of sod, sometimes plastered over to keep down the damp and dirt. When in a hurry, settlers carved "dugouts" into the hillsides facing away from prevailing northerly winds. They dug as deep as they wanted to go, then walled up the open side with sod and used what wood was available to roof it over, often placing a sod covering on top. The result was crude, leaky, dank, and prone to infestation. When it rained, rivulets of mud coursed inside, but it was better than sleeping in the open.

When more time afforded and better sod was available, the pioneers built free-standing houses, sometimes of considerable size and durability. They cut the sod in the spring with a special plow, slicing it into strips, which were then cut into large blocks or "bricks" a foot wide, and eighteen inches long, and perhaps three inches thick. To build an average soddie required about an acre of turf. They looked for sod that had a thick mat of grass growing on it, ensuring an even thicker tangle of roots beneath that acted as a "mortar" in holding the bricks together. As the walls dried, the roots kept the earth from breaking apart; thus, the older it became, the stronger the house. The most expensive part of a sod house were the windows, which could cost about $1.25—the price of an acre of public land. Then there was the lumber for the roof, which had to support the weight of the sod laid over the top. Here was the principal weak part of the house, for after some years the wood would rot or the weight of the sod would bow the roof down dangerously. The walls could last almost forever. The soddie was cool in the high plains heat and virtually immune to fire. Moreover, it was adaptable. If the settler became prosperous, it was easy to expand the house by building on new wings and cutting doors through walls. A more conventional timber and shingle roof could be added, and even standard woodframe rooms tacked on. To beautify the interior, walls were plastered with mud, smoothed down, and painted with lime whitewash. Many became so attached to their soddies that they chose to live out their days in their earthen homes. Those who found timber available—more likely from a local sawmill than freestanding on the largely treeless plains—quickly built crude frame dwellings.

The stove was essential, both for cooking and for heat in the winter. Most typical was the "ten-plate" stove specially built in the East for western use, most of them cast in the iron furnaces of Pennsylvania. With wood scarce finding something to burn required some ingenuity. Sometimes the thick dried sod would burn after a fashion, rather like the peat that the Irish knew so well. Better still were tightly packed twists of prairie grass or, after the first year's crop was in, cornstalks and cobs. Most plentiful of all, however, were buffalo chips and cattle droppings—dried animal dung.

The prairie and plains settler turned his attention to other vital matters as soon as his first rude shelter went up, and sometimes even before. He had to get the soil working for him right away. Since most immigrants went west in the spring or summer, a goodly portion of the planting and growing season was over by the time they reached their new homes. They had to race to get their parcel cleared of rocks, debris and even the few trees, and get their seed in to the ground. Farmer, plow, and ox or mule teams worked from before dawn until last twilight to break the sod, tear up the tangle of roots, and expose the virgin earth beneath. The farmers brought the seed for the crops they had known back home, chiefly corn and wheat, with a scattering of other grains depending on the soil and needs. Then followed plows and reapers that first brought West names like John Deere and McCormick, dropped their precious seed in the furrows, and waited for sun and rain and fate to bring them a crop.

The toil of a farmer on the prairie and plains was little different from that back in the East, with the added danger of sporadic Indian raids, and the drawback of isolation and a less friendly environment. Men and women performed reasonably well-defined work roles, though definitions were often blurred by the simple need to get things done. Men and older boys worked the fields and tended to the heavier livestock. Women and younger children looked after the family garden, the chickens and pigs, and all the domestic chores. Life on the plains was crushingly hard for women, and the labor wore down the frail all too quickly. Besides the constant carrying and fetching, there was the tedium of lonely prairie nights and homesickness. "I saw a vast expanse of prairie country in sunset," wrote a Kansas farm wife, "but it looked so very lonesome, and so I cried, in a moment of longing for my family so far away."

In such environment, the fellowship and company of others, however rude and unrefined, were relished by the new westerners, and they took advantage of every chance for gathering. As soon as churches formed, dozens of settlers became attendees, regardless of their former denominations. Prayer meetings, barn raisings, and quilting bees were opportunities to socialize and exchange gossip. Even more savored were the days of celebration. The Fourth of July; the harvest party that signaled the end of the season; the passing through of traveling medicine shows, dramatic troupes, even lectures, lyceums, and debates—all produced an inevitable picnic and an afternoon of respite from the grueling routine of the farm. It is no wonder that religious revivals and temperance meetings had such a profound effect on the frontier, giving fundamental ideals their deepest rooting in the sparsely settled regions of the Midwest. Frontier people needed these social occasions to keep them sane. Death and tragedy were constant companions, and all the calamities the Almighty could send hit the new westerners repeatedly in the battle between man and the land.

Towns were few at first, generally growing up as small clusters of shacks around the major trading posts, army forts, and overland-trail river crossings. But as the railroad came through and started spreading its tentacles out in an ever-expanding pattern, hundreds of new towns sprouted alongside it. There was no concept of town planning; people simply built where it suited them, usually in a straight line along a single street, usually fronting the railroad or trail—it is no accident that almost every frontier town had at its center a Front Street. If not by the railroad, the farm town was likely to be found beside a river. Towns grew in spurts and cycles, some governed by the changes in the westward movement itself, others dictated by the eastern economy, fluctuations of drought, and particularly by the success or failure of speculators who made and lost fortunes in persuading immigrants to choose one place over another. Other urban frontier towns grew up near the admirable natural harbors on the west coast and at the mining sites during the Gold Rush. These overnight cities suffered from the "boom or bust" phenomenon; men and women who came to get rich quick either did or they moved on, creating an unstable and at

times troubled local society. Hundreds of small hamlets would achieve a modest size and then remain static for generations, having fulfilled the natural limits of population imposed by what the land and the local economy would support.

Spaced at roughly twenty-mile intervals along the main travel routes, towns provided overnight stops at the end of each day's journey; the local farmers needed no more than half a day in the wagon to reach town for supplies or to sell a crop. Almost all frontier towns went through the same phases of development. First was the shabby collection of wooden buildings, designed for shelter and ready utility and devoid of style or symmetry. Tiny one-level affairs were stuffed in between the bigger structures. The only building of imposing stature was the principal hotel. False fronts rising up to a second-story roof level became popular, for no practical purpose other than to give an impression of greater size and importance. A few churches and a school, and some saloons on the outskirts, completed the picture of the unplanned community. Houses ringed the business section, usually one- and two-story frame buildings, perhaps with a porch around the street sides and a stable in the rear. If fortune smiled and the rough-and-tumble town prospered, the ensuing years witnessed a gradual attempt to give the place a greater sense of permanence and appearance of solidity. Brick and stone blocks replaced the wooden structures. Houses were built of masonry, and streets were paved with brick or cobblestones. Street lamps went up, and an unused block was turned into a park or town square; even the saloons and beer halls took on a more genteel air with marble topped mahogany bars, etched-glass doors and windows, and gas lighting. A feature of the larger and more prosperous towns was the considerable size of their transient population, a fact demonstrated by the number and size of hotels. Many people on the frontier were on the move, including salesmen, speculators, and gamblers; moreover, hotels were home to residents either unwilling or unable to rent or buy a proper house. Room rates included all meals, eaten communally in the dining room. A small society grew up within each establishment, and this compact form of community suited many who had come from the large urban centers of the East. Young married couples, single professional men, widows and spinsters often favored such accommodations—it gave them a place to belong.

The cow-town image on the raw frontier began to disappear by the mid-1880s as civic pride and political reform of the local farmers drove the lawless elements out of town. Saloons and brothels were closed, and churches came to outnumber drinking halls; theaters and an occasional opera house opened their doors in the march of eastern culture, reflecting the inevitable triumph of a civilization men and women thought they had left behind. Stimulated largely by the 1863 Morrill Act, every state obtained grants of federal land to build state universities; in the final three decades of the nineteenth century, more colleges and universities were founded west of the Mississippi than had previously existed in the East. So great was the confidence in the future that some schools were founded where there was not yet sufficient population to provide students, but almost every frontier state and territory would claim its university town as the new "Athens of the West." Religion spread with great speed and penetration, and almost from the first the churches contributed to the expansion of education. So did a flourishing press. Town newspapers gave vent to every conceivable opinion, stimulating the minds and emotions of the people. Thus the sweep across the continent that began with the wispy tracks of the wanderers and explorers grew steadily into a more deeply rutted road as the opportunists came and went on their way to elusive riches, and the settlers followed in train, putting down their roots and staking their lives on their claims. In the short span of less than a century, the West that they had originally imagined was found, realized, conquered, and then lost to legend and myth by the coming of community.

Winning the West with Railroads

By 1893, five railroads spanned the West, ranging from the Great Northern, which ran cross country between Minneapolis and St. Paul to Seattle just south of the Canadian border, to the New Orleans–Los Angeles route of the Southern Pacific. As people followed the rails, the West grew. Except for Utah, Oklahoma, Arizona, and New Mexico, every territory in the once-daunting land between the Missouri River and California became a state during the three decades of building transcontinental rail lines. The product of enormous physical labor and swashbuckling financial enterprise, the railroads were much more than mere transportation. They embodied the hope of a new beginning for settlers and offered mystery and adventure to wayfarers. In 1879, the Scottish author Robert Louis Stevenson kept a journal of his ride from Omaha to San Francisco; he complained of the cramped third-class cars with their hard wooden seats, but he found the plains strangely mesmerizing: "It was a world almost without feature," he wrote. "An empty sky, an empty earth, front and back, the line of the railway stretched from horizon to horizon. On either hand, the green plain ran till it touched the skirts of heaven." The railroads were a tremendous economic boon. Their construction created jobs and fueled a prodigious demand for raw materials. Once completed, they gave western resources easy access to eastern and European markets. As settlers rode the rails west, the trains returned to the East laden with timber, minerals, and cattle.

In the era of the Civil War, a swift advance of farming occurred across the prairie province and into the Great Plains. The outer edge of civilization advanced despite the strains and fatalities of the war in the South, an indication of the material strength of the North. The rapid spread of population meant that the Middle West between 1860 and 1880 became an enormous grain-growing community. Corn and wheat were established in these years as the great staple crops of the Midwest, and the machine age of agriculture may be said to have reached this region in the years immediately preceding the Civil War and during the war. The most important farm machine combined the reaper and binder, uniting the functions of cutting the ripe wheat in the fields and binding it. Another great improvement was a plow made of chilled steel, which was put on the market in 1868; this was a light and tough instrument, admirably suited to breaking the prairie sod. Other agricultural machines came in quick succession: machines for drilling seeds into the ground, corn planters, corn huskers, and scores of others.

They produced a revolution in farming comparable in extent and in significance to the Industrial Revolution, which was transforming the urban production of the United States in the same years. Its effect was to neutralize the high labor costs of the West, which had been one of the chief handicaps in competing in the food markets of the world.

In 1860, the United States were united in name only. Besides the nation's growing split over slavery, the young states of California and Oregon lay divided from the rest of the country by a vast sweep of wilderness populated mainly by Indians, Mexicans, and a few buffalo hunters, prospectors, and pioneering farmers. For many Americans, this territory was the unfinished business of Manifest Destiny. They dreamed of conquering the wilderness and spreading American civilization throughout the West. Traveling across the country was a daunting task; between the Missouri River and California's settled coast lay some 1,600 miles of intimidating prairie, desert, and mountains. Seldom has any human undertaking presented more difficult and dangerous natural obstacles than those faced by the surveyors, engineers, and track-laying gangs of the Union Pacific and Central Pacific railroads as they built the first rail line across the West. The greatest obstacle to the building of a transcontinental railroad was the Sierra Nevada Mountains. Running almost the entire length of the state of California and isolating the populous coastal cities from the rest of the continent, the Sierra was held by conventional wisdom to be impassable to trains. Two hardheaded, practical visionaries who more than any others realized the stupendous dream of pushing a railroad across the West were a remarkable pair of New England–born engineers, Theodore Judah and Grenville M. Dodge. Ignoring the clamor of doubters who thought him crazy, Judah pushed ahead single-handedly, surveying a usable route from California eastward through a gradually rising pass through the Sierras. He then helped put together the financial package that made the track-laying possible. Dodge, equally dedicated and tireless, spent almost five years alone on the western plains surveying a rail route westward from Missouri to the Rockies and then commanded the army of construction workers that thrust the Union Pacific tracks to a

meeting with the Central Pacific line that Judah had planned and foreseen. Crews had to construct bridges long enough to span the wide floor plains of great rivers and high enough for steamboat smokestacks to pass underneath; they risked their lives working a hundred feet or more above canyon floors to build spidery wooden trestles and they sweated and died carving ledges to carry tracks high along sheer canyon walls and cutting their way through miles of heavy rock, especially to get to the Rockies. Toughest of all were the many tunnels that had to be driven straight through mountains, such as the Summit Tunnel beneath the Donner Pass in the Sierras—a twenty-foot-high bore drilled and blasted through 1,659 feet of solid granite.

As the pace of construction quickened, the spot selected where the iron band binding West and East would be completed was Promontory Summit, about fifty miles east of Ogden in the hills north of the Great Salt Lake. To great hoopla and wild rejoicing, ceremonial golden spikes were driven down to hold down the last rail, and the cowcatchers of two locomotives loaded with dignitaries touched, completing the two-thousand-mile line spanning the West from Omaha to Sacramento. All in all, the construction of the first transcontinental railroad, and the other lines that followed, ranks as the greatest technological triumph of its day. In 1870, its first full year of operation, nearly 150,000 passengers rode the line; a dozen years later, the number soared to almost a million. For most Americans, the railroads meant the transformation of the West from forbidding wilderness to land of opportunity. The haunting train whistle calling across the endless prairie symbolized commerce, safety, speed, and civilization. It created the somehow soothing feeling that the West and the cultured East were finally, truly, the United States.

"Cheap lands! Easily cultivated! Inexhaustible fertility," trumpeted the land promoters. Crowds of people responded, some literally galloping into huge areas opened up by the railroads. More lastingly, the railroads made huge granaries of the once forbidding wilderness. Survey teams routinely struck out ahead of tracklaying crews to choose townsites from the millions of acres the federal government had granted to the railroads. The locations were then plotted and sold to offset the huge costs of the transcontinental project. Speculators swarmed close behind the surveying parties, hoping to buy when the tracks were still far from town and land prices low, and to sell when the lines approached and prices soared. As rough-and-tumble towns were built gold and silver prospectors in Colorado and Nevada, loggers in Oregon, and buffalo hunters and cattle ranchers in Kansas, immigrants, freed slaves, prohibitionists, vegetarians, religious utopians, and other groups were also founding towns. And cities were blossoming capriciously along numerous wagon trails and steamboat routes simply because the sites proved to be convenient stopping places for westering travelers. The result was a network of communities as diverse as all America. Congress touched off the building boom by making the formation of such towns relatively easy, and profitable. Under the terms of the Federal Townsite Act of 1867, a group of one hundred or more settlers could form a so-called township company by obtaining a charter from a territorial or state legislature. Then, for $400, or $1.25 an acre, they could withdraw 320 acres from the federal domain and take possession. Once a few additional legal requirements were met, most companies wasted little time in commissioning a surveying team to make a town plan. They divided the land into salable units, creating a neat grid of streets and blocks that reproduced well in printed promotional materials. This was no small consideration for those entrepreneurs—known as "boomers" after the building boom they hoped to set off—who began towns purely as speculative ventures. Their task was a stiff one: to persuade eastern settlers to buy lots in a frontier town, even though in almost every instance the municipality existed only on paper and in the dreams of its founders.

But appearances could be deceiving. The colorful brochures described a thriving metropolis with wide avenues, fine residences, a machine shop, hotel, schools, and churches, with train tracks running through the town's center, but new arrivals soon discovered there was little more than a muddy street, a few general stores, and some ramshackle dwellings. But mendacity did not defeat the hardy; in time, most swallowed their losses, packed up again, and moved on to another promising frontier town.

Such courage was a virtue born of necessity because disappointments were many on the frontier. Fires were a routine disaster, and prairie fires savaged many a farming community. Cholera, typhoid, diphtheria, and other scourges beset westerners because of terrible sanitation and a lack of qualified doctors. Yet, even the most godforsaken frontier communities stood at least a fighting chance of making it, provided that they started out with certain essential citizens. Next to a blacksmith, the most important of these was the newspaper editor. A hotelier and a saloon keeper, partners in accommodating and entertaining wayfarers and prospective settlers, were also vital. More often than not, however, the proprietor of the general store became the town's most popular figure. He sold not only guns and chaps, bootjacks and baby carriages, but also Bibles for the devout and whiskey for the sinners. Few frontier communities were fortunate enough to start out with the full array of skills and talents that contributed to the convenience of life back East. Most made do with the bare minimum and advertised for services that were missing. "What we want now most is mechanics," pleaded the *Kansas Weekly Herald* in 1854, at a time when the word mechanic was used to describe any skilled artisan. "We have several kinds but not enough of them. We have not got a Saddler, Shoemaker, Tailor, Cabinet Maker, Hatter, nor Milliner in the place." Until such specialists arrived, most towns relied on the resourcefulness and versatility of their citizens.

By 1870, railroads had crossed the wheat belt of Minnesota and the corn belt of Iowa and Missouri and were moving into the Great Plains. At the same time, a revolution was occurring in the methods of grain handling in the transfer centers of the West. It was the elevator system, specialized structures for the handling and storing of grain some with a capacity of millions of bushels. Grain elevators consisted of a series of tall, perpendicular bins into which grain of predetermined grade was hoisted by buckets on endless belts; carloads could be elevated into a bin in a few minutes, and all the economies of mass handling became possible. Another institution—the so-called futures trading—was developed in the 1860s in the Middle West, while the new methods of transportation and marketing of grain were of major advantage to the farmers of the Mid West, making possible effective competition with grain markets of Great Britain and continental Europe. This immense addition to the production of food occurred when great increases were being made in Canada, South America, and Australia. Agricultural overproduction became a worldwide phenomenon and with it came steadily sagging farm prices. The twenty years between 1877 and 1897 were a period of ruinously low prices for farm produce and intense distress for farmers, not only in the United States, but also around the world. In the late 1880s, a major reversal of the climatic cycle occurred, resulting in a dry cycle of greater than normal intensity, which added its woes to the troubles of the farmers on the Great Plains and the cotton South. The magnitude of the disaster and evils undermining rural life became evident in a political disturbance alarming to the nation in 1890s, a disturbance known as Populism.

The westward movement across the continent was not only prolonged but massive, bringing uncounted millions from the Old World to the New, and from the shores of the Atlantic to the Pacific. It was the greatest migration of peoples in recorded history. It was magnificent in its achievements. It replaced barbarism with civilization. It unlocked the bounties of nature and made them a blessing to mankind. It bent reluctant and unfriendly forces of nature to man's will and control. It created a nation that has given leadership to the free peoples of the world. It gave the nation many of its fundamental democratic institutions. It helped shape American literature and art, sectional and national, and imparted emotional and spiritual values to successive generations. To them, the open West was the land of promise, the utopia of their dreams.

Some aspects of the movement were less attractive. Conquest, speculation, exploitation, and violence were all part of this crusade into the wilderness. They were the harsher realities of the movement and the source of some of the nation's present problems. They were a reflection of a dynamic society, determined in the face of resistance, rising on successive frontiers from youth to maturity. The whole story of westward expansion has been called the frontier process by Frederick Jackson Turner and dubbed the continental lure by Bernard De Voto.

In 1890, after almost thirty years of settlement abetted by the generous terms of the Homestead Act, steamboat travel, improved roads, and new rail lines, precious little of the West remained unclaimed. In fact, there were so many people residing between the Mississippi River and the Pacific Ocean, the director of the Bureau of the Census announced that the frontier as a continuous line no longer existed. That observation was the point of departure for the great essay of Frederick Jackson Turner, "The Significance of the Frontier in American History," given at the Chicago World's Columbian Exposition in 1893. That essay has been misread by some as saying that the frontier in all aspects had ended. But in a sense, the frontier still exists in the persistent notion that somehow the West is a symbol of the American future. The hope is that all the optimism, all the indomitable will to overcome obstacles, all the love of freedom and of democratic process, and all the determination to make things better for the future, which the old frontier nourished and symbolized, is an integral part of American thought and aspiration.

The Age of Expansion
in the
Frontier West

opposite
Lobby of the Osborne, a New York City apartment house in the Renaissance revival style, built by Thomas Osborne and decorated by Jacob Adolphous Holzer, 1883–85.

Brass and tile fireplace surround in an apartment in the Osborne. Every fireplace in the building has an elaborate cast-iron fireback and is faced with colorful ceramic tiles and *repoussé* brass. Fireplaces in American homes had been adorned with blue-and-white tin-glazed earthenware tiles from Holland and England since Colonial days. Now, in the Aesthetic period, decorative tiles became almost a requirement in stylish households, enriching foyers and floors as well as fireplaces.

Vestibule of the Osborne. The ceiling is decorated with round and other geometric relief reserves; the floor is primarily mosaic with some marble. The patterned walls and ceiling of this spectacular vestibule, polychromed and textured in a variety of rich materials, were part of the art-decoration movement in America in the 1870s and 1880s. Exponents of art decoration generally emphasized handcrafted as opposed to mass-produced objects, subtle colors rather than the harsh hues characteristic of mid-century synthetic dyes, the desirability of eliminating superfluous ornament, and the notion that beauty results from an object's fitness for its purpose. This grand vestibule was conceived as a place to view and to pass through, not as a living space.

The forty-seven-ton Caen-stone mantel in the model room of the New York Yacht Club, New York City, built between 1898 and 1901. Organized in 1844, the New York Yacht Club built this clubhouse on land contributed by Commodore J. Pierpont Morgan in 1898. It was designed by Whitney Warren and Charles Devon Wetmore—a six-story building on Forty-fourth Street, reminiscent of ships and the sea in every possible way. The painting inset in the mantel is by Julius L. Stewart.

Olana, the eclectic, picturesque villa of the Hudson River school painter Frederic Edwin Church, Hudson, New York. Begun in 1870 and occupied by the family in 1872, when Church was at the peak of his success as a landscape painter, Olana, a dramatic composite of Western and Near Eastern architecture, was to be Church's personal expression of exotic eclecticism. The house was designed by the artist in consultation with architects Calvert Vaux and Frederick Clarke Withers. The studio wing at the left was built between 1888 and 1891. Olana crowns a hilltop overlooking the Hudson River and the Catskill Mountains beyond—the sort of panoramic vista that Church painted in his mammoth canvases.

opposite

Stair hall of Olana. Church brought back from abroad not simply the idea for a Moorish house; his travels also inspired in him the desire and confidence to create the house and its interior himself. Colorful stenciling, derived from plates of Eastern ornament, frames the arches. Concentrated in the stair hall are some of Church's finest objets d'art, including Persian rugs, brassware, armor, and a gold, wood and gesso Buddha. To him, Olana was "the Center of the World." And, he added, "I own it."

236

Sitting room of Olana. The key to understanding the colors and stencils of the house is found in the court hall, the visual and artistic center of the house. The colors of the court hall's walls and stencils radiate to the adjoining rooms. The salmon color found at the edge of the broad Islamic arches in the court hall, for example, reappears here in the sitting room—in the window and door embrasures, in the marble fireplace front, and in *El Khasné, Petra,* Church's painting of 1874 (completed in 1875) depicting an ancient treasury house carved from stone that is the visual focus of the room. The salmon color reappears on the exterior cornices and on the column capitals of the piazza. Certainly, Olana's effect on some visitors was a sense of Middle Eastern fantasy. As one visiting journalist concluded in 1889, "One feels as if transported into the Orient when surrounded by so much Eastern magnificence."

East parlor of Olana. The architectural design of the house is neither in the villa style typical of the work of Andrew Jackson Downing, nor is it a Gothic-style castle; it is Near Eastern in feeling. It is an astonishing mélange of color, texture, and form brought into harmony and order by the overall patterning, the blending of hues and tones controlling the eye as it moves from object to object.

Studio at Olana. In 1888, Church's renewed interest in the house culminated in the construction of a three-story wing that included, in addition to the studio, a gallery, observatory, bedroom, and storage room. Constructed of the same materials as the villa, the studio wing required three years to complete and cost $30,000. He wrote: "I wonder if I shall work as hard in the new Studio as I do in erecting it."

Dining room and picture gallery of Olana, which
displays the collection of Old Master paintings
Church gathered in Europe during 1868 and 1869.
The rooms of Olana were filled with exotic objects:
painted Kashmiri tables and chairs, Shaker rockers,
rococo revival furniture inherited from his father, and
furniture built to Church's own designs were
intermingled with Persian and Syrian metalware,
Mexican religious statuary, mounted South American
birds and butterflies, marble and bronze statuary by
Erastus Dow Palmer, and Turkish rugs. Most of the
objects that comprise Olana's exotic diversity have
little intrinsic value; rather, Church selected objects
in part for their visual and associative effects. These
artifacts have an iconographic significance; they
were physical and symbolic expressions of ancient
cultures and religions.

Entrance hall of Three Fountain Place, Ithaca, New York, begun in the 1840s as a Greek cottage, enlarged as a Gothic cottage in 1851 by the owner Francis Miles Finch, and remodeled in 1874 to 1875 in the Queen Anne style by the architect William Henry Miller. The walnut and dark-stained staircase, anchored by an impressive newel post of coupled columns surmounted by a *torchère* of fantastic birds, ascends along the angled walls of the dramatic entrance hall. The flat patterns of the stained and painted glass reflect the reform attitudes of English "artistic" designers such as Charles Locke Eastlake and his American disciple, Clarence Cook.

Library of Three Fountain Place. The library was the soul of the house for Francis Finch, housing his collection of contemporary journals and literary volumes. It was as a lawyer that Finch came to know Ezra Cornell, for whom he was personal attorney, trusted adviser, and lifelong friend; in 1895, he became the dean of the Cornell Law School. Finch received numerous offers of literary professorships, all of which he declined, at one point explaining: "My whole life as a lawyer has been a battle against literary longings. I have kept the most earnest part of my nature in chains." His dual callings are reflected in the Arundel Society prints after Raphael—figures of Justice and Poetry—which were the gift of Cornell's first president, Andrew Dickson White. Between them, on the mantel shelf, is an Ithaca calendar clock.

The George S. Batcheller mansion, Saratoga Springs, New York, designed by the architects Nichols and Halcott of Albany and built in 1871–73. The flamboyant and eclectic house combines the picturesque elements of a bracketed porch and Italianate lower floors with French-inspired, shell-incised window heads on the dormers, a sharply pitched mansard roof, and a conical tower topped by a medieval turret, inspired by the châteaus of the Loire River valley. Saratoga Springs, located in the foothills of the Adirondack Mountains, became a fashionable resort because of the therapeutic properties of its mineral waters. Well into the nineteenth century, life in Saratoga Springs centered on the grand hotels, which catered to wealthy Europeans and Americans with European pretensions, especially Southerners eager to escape the summer heat. Henry James visited Saratoga Springs in 1870 and was horrified by its "monster" hotels. He felt the resort was too openly commercial, too harsh, too urban, too worldly, with no sense of community.

overleaf
The parlor of the Theodore Roosevelt Birthplace,
New York City, built in 1848. In 1916, when Theodore
Roosevelt died, the Women's Roosevelt Memorial
Association came into being and decided to
commemorate the twenty-sixth president by
reconstructing and furnishing the house in which he
was born. The date chosen for the restoration was
1865, the year in which the elder Roosevelts hired
Léon Marcotte to refurbish the house.

The library or back parlor of the Theodore Roosevelt
Birthplace. Roosevelt later recalled that it was the
family living room and filled with "chairs, tables, and
bookcases of gloomy respectability." The senior
Roosevelts brought back the obelisks on the mantel
from a trip to Egypt in 1868. The Argand lamp on the
center table was supplied with gas from the overhead
fixture, as was customary in the last century.

Dining room of the Theodore Roosevelt Birthplace. The walnut chairs with horsehair upholstery were a wedding present to Roosevelt's parents-in-law, Charles and Gertrude Carow, who were married in 1853. The walnut dining table belonged to Roosevelt's grandfather Cornelius. The cornices here and throughout the house were molded in place in 1923. The ceiling rosette, chimneypiece, and fireplace grate were salvaged from mid-nineteenth-century houses in the process of being demolished. The house on Twentieth Street, with its heavy brocade draperies, dark furniture, and horsehair sofas and chairs, had an air of serene gentility. No one had a greater influence upon his namesake than the high-minded Theodore, Sr., by example and instruction imbuing Theodore, Jr., with a strong sense of moral values. "My father . . . was the best man I ever knew," he often declared. "He was the only man of whom I was ever really afraid."

The Ebenezer Maxwell Mansion. Built of local Wissahickon schist and red sandstone, the house combines a number of architectural styles. The French doors on the porch open into the parlor, and the round windows in the gables are at floor level on the third story. The house incorporated what were then the latest modern conveniences: gas lighting, hot-air central heating, and hot and cold running water. The Maxwell Mansion is the only Victorian house museum in Philadelphia, a city that emphasizes its eighteenth-century heritage.

Parlor of the Ebenezer Maxwell Mansion. Maxwell was a prosperous but not wealthy businessman, and his taste for mass-produced sets of furniture in the rococo and Renaissance revival styles is reflected in the furnishings of the house. The mahogany card table by the door, rocking chair, and pair of side chairs by the window belonged to the Maxwell family. The mahogany armchair in the center of the room retains its original upholstery and, according to family tradition, belonged to the lawyer and statesman Richard Rush, son of Benjamin Rush. The marble-topped mahogany center table is a fine example of the rococo revival style as realized in Philadelphia. None of the floors in the house have been finished, indicating that since the beginning they have been carpeted wall to wall. The carpet was woven in Scotland by a firm that still retained its nineteenth-century loom cards. The wallpaper is a reproduction of a period paper in the collection of the Cooper-Hewitt Museum in New York City.

One of a pair of painted and grained sliding doors that separate two bedrooms on the second floor of the Ebenezer Maxwell Mansion. The woodwork of the house was painted and grained, as advocated by Downing in *The Architecture of Country Houses*. The woodwork in the parlor was grained to resemble walnut, and that in the front hall to resemble oak. It is believed that the second-floor rooms were redecorated in the 1870s with handsome stenciled and freehand patterns.

opposite
Dining room of the Ebenezer Maxwell Mansion. The walnut serving table at the right and the round walnut extension table and walnut arm and side chairs around it were made about 1860 by the Lajambre firm in Philadelphia and are on loan from a descendant of the cabinetmaker. The chandelier is similar to one shown in the 1859 catalog of the Archer, Warner and Miskey Company of Philadelphia. The gilded looking glass on the mantelpiece is marked by Archer and Warner of Philadelphia and is stamped with the patent date of 1852. The wallpaper is copied from a period document found in the Gallier House in New Orleans.

Drawing room of the Reitz Home, Evansville, Indiana. The clutter of furnishings of all sorts associated with the Victorian domestic scene was in part a consequence of the rising productivity and spreading affluence of the period. As in this drawing room, articles fabricated or ornamented by machinery could be less expensively produced than handmade objects; following the Civil War, the machine had in good measure replaced the craftsman working by hand who had provided the wants of people for time out of mind. A spate of books, magazine articles, and newspaper reports issued from the presses to guide the homemaker in matters of taste and economy in architecture, furnishing, and interior decoration.

opposite
Parlor of the Reitz Home, built for John Augustus Reitz in 1871. Reitz made his fortune in the lumber business along the Ohio River, and built this elegant and spacious Italianate villa, an exuberant example of mansard architecture, to reflect his station in life. The stucco-over-brick structure has heavy window and cornice details and elongated roof brackets. The interior, with its painted ceilings, is furnished with American antiques in the rococo, Renaissance, and Louis XVI revival styles. The eldest son, Francis Joseph Reitz, took over the house after his parents' deaths in the 1890s and redecorated the home's interior in a variety of eclectic Victorian styles. The 1890s atmosphere haunting the parlor, appearing much as it did a hundred years ago, has been retained in accordance with the wishes of the last of John Augustus Reitz's children, who died in 1931.

Library of the Reitz Home. Among the rich mélange of wall decorations typifying high Victorian design, imported simulated leather of embossed canvas was particularly popular, as seen here. Among American firms, one Boston factory offered "reproductions of the rare old illuminated leathers of the Moors, the Spaniards and Venetians." Tastemakers generally advocated a tripartite arrangement for wall and ceiling treatment of three horizontal divisions in rooms: the wainscot, or dado; the fill, or upper wall; and the partial entablature of the cornice and sometimes a frieze. Decorating experts warned of the danger of the excess of ornamentation, as on walls like these that could be perceived as a place for painted decorations.

opposite

Bedroom of the Reitz Home. The Civil War accelerated developments that were revolutionizing the nature of the American economy and the very structure of American society. In the turmoil of modernity, Americans with nostalgia looked backward to stained glass—a medieval art form— during the aesthetic movement to be used in secular settings in home decoration, endowing the home with a hallowed quality. It was especially desirable for library windows, but it was also useful for vestibules, hall windows, stair landings, fan lights, and doors of bookcases and cabinets. Stained glass could form the upper sash, as it does here, and veil the prospect of a lifeless wall.

The Pabst Mansion, Milwaukee, Wisconsin. The Pabst Mansion has no equal in Milwaukee or elsewhere in the Midwest. Built between 1890 and 1892 in the Flemish Renaissance revival style, the mansion is the crowning residential project of the architect George Bowman Ferry of Ferry and Clas. With interest in the American Renaissance revival peaking at the 1893 Chicago World Columbian Exposition, Pabst was leading the aesthetic reaction against Victorian Gothic and Eastlake architecture characteristic of Milwaukee in the 1880s. Ferry abandoned towers, turrets, and architectural gimcrackery to design this house of great dignity with its symmetrical facade, arcaded loggia, and exterior enriched with seventeenth-century Renaissance forms of Flemish and German derivation. Constructed of tan pressed brick and terra-cotta ornament, the house is distinguished by its stepped gables on the front elevation with volutes, scrollwork, and the lion insignia in a decorative panel.

opposite
Parlor of the Pabst Mansion. The interior design of the parlor is French rococo in style. The shell motif that occurs throughout the room harmonizes with flourishes, garlands, and scrollwork. The rococo fireplace mantel is carved in onyx marble. The parlor was the place for intimate evening salons, often preferred by the ladies as a place of retreat and conversation following a dinner party. The parlor of the Pabst Mansion illustrates that indiscriminate mixture of design sources of the late nineteenth century, of classical and rococo details with Renaissance design.

overleaf
Reception hall of the Pabst Mansion, fitted with ceremonial chairs, statuary, paintings, and an enormous gas and electric chandelier. The woodwork, paneling, and mantel of the hall are in golden oak in the German Renaissance style. The paneling and woodwork in intricately crafted oak are clearly of German design, and the rest of the interior is compatibly embellished with marble-lined fireplaces and ornamental plaster. Early reports state that the mansion was equipped with every possible luxury and convenience, including a three-story passenger elevator, an attached plant conservatory, separate parlors for the men and ladies, a billiard room, a wine cellar, and a porte cochere over the driveway.

Dining room of the Pabst Mansion. The dining room is in the rococo revival style, in which the shell motif complements the rose and floral festoon and scrollwork. The woodwork and furniture in the Louis XV style are attributed to the Matthews brothers, a noted Milwaukee cabinetry company. The flourishes and embellishments of the ceiling were inspired by Renaissance decorative patterns.

overleaf

Corner cabinetry of golden birch and maple in the dining room of the Pabst Mansion. The cabinets with their rounded hoods show the influence of the baroque style. Pabst's residence is the quintessential German beer baron's mansion, built at a staggering cost by a self-confident millionaire whose bold choice of an eclectic architectural style defied local tradition. The architectural decoration of the dining room was in the grand French manner. Pabst's taste for the good life included a well-stocked wine cellar.

overleaf, and opposite

Music room of the Pabst Mansion. In his music room, Pabst entertained his guests with performances by popular singers who were accompanied on his Steinway piano. The architectural style of the room was influenced by the Venetian Renaissance, with its massive mahogany entablatures over the doorways and fireplace, and the elaborately spiraled columns and Corinthian capitals that are characteristic of the style. The fireplace is faced with Carrara marble from Italy. The elaborate pressed ceiling with its repetition is anaglypta, or pressed paper, an innovation of that time.

272

Marble fireplace in the Louis XV style in the W. H. Stark House, Orange, Texas, built about 1894 and possibly designed by Fred Wilbur of Williamsport, Pennsylvania, an uncle by marriage of Mrs. Stark. The "line of beauty," as William Hogarth called the serpentine curve of the eighteenth century, was the basis for the design of this fireplace, symmetrical and balanced in plan, with its bold and typically rococo cartouche flanked by S-curve forms. The incised diapered pattern on the breast is common to the nineteenth century.

opposite
Stairwell of the Stark House. Surface ornament, to use a popular term of the late nineteenth century, seemed to cover everything in American rooms deemed beautiful: patterns on walls, ceilings, carpets and rugs, window draperies, portieres, pillows, and upholstery dominated all of the available space. But turn-of-the-century tastemakers, in campaigning for the purity and authority of historical styles, soon rejected the visual complexity in interior decoration of the eccentric, eclectic patterns of earlier decades. Edith Wharton in *The Decoration of Houses* (1897) and Elsie de Wolfe in *The House in Good Taste* (1911) popularized and embellished this understanding of "good taste" in interior decorating in America.

Doorway of the Stark House. The three-story, fifteen-room, wood-frame structure—with its many gables and galleries and a distinctive windowed turret—shows the influence of several late-Victorian revival styles. The asymmetrical Stark House was built in what was called the Queen Anne style of architecture. At the end of the nineteenth century the style was transformed into the American vernacular, characterized by light frame construction, irregular picturesque outlines, sharply peaked roofs, spindled verandas, upper-story balconies, and large, open, interior spaces. Such buildings, with their open halls and great fireplaces recalling Elizabethan and Jacobean structures, were felt to be "sincere," "artistic," and "practical," and at the same time a fitting complement to Eastlake furnishings.

Dining room of the Stark House with an appropriate display of silver.

Sitting room of Villa Finale. The gilded cornices above the windows came from a plantation house on the Mississippi River. The late nineteenth-century washstand is a copy of the one Empress Josephine used at Malmaison.

opposite
Villa Finale, an Italianate house subsequently owned by the rancher Edwin Polk and the celebrated trail boss and cattleman, Ike T. Pryor. The bold opulence of the mansion suggests something of the prosperity that accompanied the arrival of the railroad in San Antonio in the late 1870s.

Upstairs kitchen of Villa Finale. The art-glass chandelier is original to the house. The southern pine cupboard of about 1878 was salvaged from the Sullivan house, which once stood on Broadway in San Antonio. The deep dish and jar on the Texas magnolia-wood table of about 1850 are Meyer pottery. The Enterprise Manufacturing Company of Philadelphia made the large coffee mill that stands in front of the refrigerator. Early kitchen tools complement the colorful array of spices, candies, and dried foods stored in apothecary jars. The kitchen epitomizes the southern hospitality remembered by Tulitas Wulff Jamieson, who wrote of her girlhood near King William Street in San Antonio: "There were cakes so light they had to be held down with inch-thick icings, rolls that vanished in your mouth like a puff of smoke, great roasts of beef with thick, delicious gravy, chicken cooked in a dozen ways, homemade bread that tasted better than any bakery ever smelled, tortes smothered in whipped cream."

overleaf

The limestone house of Edward Steves, Jr., on King William Street in San Antonio, Texas, designed by James Wahrenberger and Albert F. Beckmann in 1883–84. Following the annexation of the Republic of Texas in 1845, San Antonio grew and prospered as a major cattle center, where herds were assembled for the long drives overland on the famous Chisholm Trail to the railroads in Kansas. The architectural excellence of King William Street and the surrounding neighborhood reflects the thrust of economic growth and restless change that marked late nineteenth-century San Antonio. By 1876 the city had grown to over seventeen thousand, a good third of German descent. When Frederick Law Olmsted took his horseback journey through Texas in 1854, he wrote of San Antonio: "The houses were evidently German, of fresh square-cut blocks of creamy white limestone, mostly of a single story and humble proportions, but neat, and thoroughly roofed and finished." The elder Edward Steves built his homestead on King William Street between 1874 and 1876, the earliest work of the Englishman Alfred Giles, in the French Second Empire and the Italian villa styles. Since it was the German custom to keep the family together, one of his sons built this house across from the original homestead.

Parlor of the Grant-Kohrs Ranch, Deer Lodge, Montana, built in 1862 by Johnny Grant and enlarged with a brick addition in 1890 by Conrad Kohrs. Dreams of wealth lured the first cattlemen to Montana. Johnny Grant—a Canadian trapper, hunter, and mountain man—built a two-story log house here in Deer Lodge Valley in 1862 for his Indian wife and large family. He worked this ranch for only a few years, sold out to Conrad Kohrs in 1866, and returned to Canada. Kohrs, a German immigrant, was a shrewd businessman in the frontier cattle business, trading and selling beef to mining camps. Kohrs brought in as breeding stock registered Shorthorns and Herefords, and under him the ranch became one of the best known in the region. In 1868 Kohrs, on a trip East, found himself a wife, the nineteen-year-old Augusta Kruse, of German background, who tried to make her home as comfortable and gracious as possible, and a good place for raising children and entertaining friends. Augusta Kohrs after her marriage settled in and brought a much-needed order and touch of culture to the primitive ranch.

overleaf

Parlor of the Grant-Kohrs Ranch. When Johnny Grant built his house on the frontier grazing lands of Montana, it was said by the *Montana Post* to be the finest house in the territory and looked as if "it had been lifted by the chimneys from the banks of the St. Lawrence and dropped down in Deer Lodge Valley. It has twenty-eight windows, with green painted shutters, and looks very pretty."

Deepwood, Salem, Oregon. Dr. Luke A. Port constructed his elegant home in the Queen Anne style in 1894, following the design of William C. Knighton, one of Salem's notable architects of the period. Elaborate in texture and irregular in plan, Deepwood has two stories, a full basement, observatory, veranda, and porte cochere modified for use as a sunporch. The foundation is made of native "pioneer" stone, a sandstone quarried at Pioneer, Oregon, on the Yanguina River near the summit of the Coast Range. The exterior is covered with clapboard and shingle siding in contrasting strata. The roof line is a complex variety of porch and dormer pediments, gable and hipped roofs, and a square bell-cast steeple or tower roof atop the observatory. The second-story cornice line is embellished by console brackets. The dressed-stone chimney exposed on the south side is treated as an important feature of the house.

Stained-glass window at Deepwood. Dr. Port had the window built in honor of his only son, Omega Port, who at the age of twenty-two drowned at sea off the Azores in 1887. The stone chimney stack is pierced by this round-arched stained-glass window, which is attributed to Povey Brothers Studio of Portland, the leading manufacturers of fine art glass in Oregon for many years.

Bush House, built from 1877–78 by the pioneer
banker and newspaper publisher Asahel Bush. A local
contractor, Wilbur F. Boothby, the builder of the old
Second Empire Baroque Marion County Court House
in Salem, is credited with the design of the house.
Italianate in style, the house has drop siding,
bracketed gable roofs, elongated windows with
segmental arch heads, a high basement, a polygonal
bay, and a veranda from which a long flight of stairs
leads to the lawn. One of the prominent figures in
Oregon history, Bush founded the *Oregon Statesman*
newspaper and later the Ladd and Bush Bank, both
of which still operate in Salem. The Victorian home
sat in the midst of a sizable estate and was the focal
point of a farm complex that included a large barn, a
much-loved greenhouse, and open ground for
pasturing cattle.

opposite
Parlor corner of the Bush House in Salem, Oregon.
Asahel Bush came to Oregon in 1850 from Westfield,
Massachusetts, and in 1853 settled in Salem, where
he became active in Democratic party politics in the
Oregon territory. His wife died in 1863, leaving him
with four young children; it was his daughter Sally,
who as a college student, traveled to Springfield,
Massachusetts, to select furniture for the house.

Italian marble mantel in the parlor of the Bush House. In the sculptural decorations of the magnificent private dwellings and civic buildings in the last quarter of the nineteenth century, the direct influence of the Ecole des Beaux-Arts is apparent. It was the period of the last great architectural revivals—the neo-Renaissance, of either the French châteaus or the Italian *palazzo* type, which in revival form came to incorporate considerable amounts of sculptural decoration. Downstairs, besides the parlor, there are a sitting room, library, master bedroom, dining room, and kitchen. A broad staircase of walnut and mahogany leads from the central entrance hall to bedrooms, sitting rooms, and servants' quarters upstairs. Ten of the twelve rooms have mantels cut in a distinctive style from imported Italian marble. The rich interior includes original embossed French wallpapers, brass fittings, and elaborate woodwork. The Renaissance revival sofa, conceived as three separate chair backs and as a single, coherent piece of furniture, is ornamented with incised lines. The tufted, three-dimensional upholstery is a foil to the flat, linear ornament of the surrounding seat and back rails.

293

The Ladd and Bush Bank Building in Salem, Oregon, constructed in 1868–69. This imposing cast-iron building was designed by the Portland architect John Nestor. The ground floor of the building includes twenty-nine semicircular arches on two facades. Each pier is sheathed with a group of three cast-iron pilasters, with the central one being the tallest and most prominent. The shafts of these taller pilasters are divided into ten rectangular units made to resemble rusticated stone masonry. Their shafts rise from a Roman Doric pedestal and base, culminating in a Composite capital with volutes, acanthus leaves, and other foliate decoration. Flanking these are two smaller and shorter pilasters, with fluted shafts rising from Roman Doric pedestals and bases to Corinthian-order capitals. The shorter pilasters are below impost blocks with egg-and-dart decorations, from which spring semicircular cast-iron arches that include five prominent protruding voussoirs decorated with volutes and floral motifs.

Parlor fireplace mantel and tile surround in the Flavel House, Astoria, Oregon, in the Eastlake style. Captain George Flavel, a pioneer Columbia River bar pilot, retained the German-born architect Carl W. Leick to design his stately Victorian mansion in 1885. Flavel, a native of Norfolk, Virginia, came to the northern Pacific coast by way of the California gold fields in 1849. The architectural elements of the house that characterize the Queen Anne style are the hipped roof with the cresting balcony, the shingled siding, and the wrap around veranda. The house has Italianate features as well, including bracketed eaves, hooded moldings above the windows, and decorative columns on the veranda. Inside the house there is elaborate Eastlake-style woodwork around the doors, windows, and staircases. This is one of six fireplace mantels, each carved from a different hardwood and each with a different tile surround, imported from craftsmen in Europe and Asia.

opposite
Chandelier and ceiling rosette in the Flavel House. Chandeliers evolved with changing styles as much as did tables and chairs, and this one, with its floral motifs, has the decoration characteristic of art furniture of the 1880s. Natural gas was one of the most revolutionary lighting sources of the nineteenth century. As early as 1851, Cornelius & Company of Philadelphia exhibited two gas chandeliers at the Crystal Palace, and the firm flourished until near the end of the century. Glass shades or globes were used to protect the burning gas jets from drafts.

Carson House, Eureka, northern California, built by William Carson, about 1888. Carson was a redwood pioneer and successful lumber magnate who may have wanted to show off the wonderful effects that could be achieved with lumber. Carson commissioned the architects Samuel and Joseph C. Newsom to build a wooden mansion next to his lumberyards in Eureka. By the time this extravaganza was raised, steam-powered woodworking machinery had taken over the production of much of the carved and turned ornamental detail that had for ages past been the province of handcraftsmen.

overleaf

The Gingerbread Mansion, Fernale, Humboldt County, in northern California. Built in 1899 as a residence for a local physician, Dr. Hogan J. Ring, the house is a combination of the Queen Anne revival and Eastlake styles, elaborately trimmed with ornate gingerbread of pleasurable fancy and exuberant color. Houses like this impressed European visitors with their conveniences and amenities. These were the first to feature central heating by warm–air furnaces, hot and cold running water, "bathrooms," cooking ranges, and indoor toilets. They also boasted high ceilings, a big kitchen, both a front and a back yard, and ample storage space in the cellar and attic.

Places of Interest

Many of the houses illustrated in this book welcome visitors. They either have official hours when they are open, or they can be seen by appointment.